Election Finance Regulation in Canada

Election Finance Regulation in Canada

A • CRITICAL • REVIEW

by Filip Palda

The Fraser Institute
Vancouver, British Columbia, Canada

The author of this book has worked independently and opinions
expressed by him, therefore, are his own, and do not necessarily
reflect the opinions of the members or the trustees of The Fraser
Institute.

Canadian Cataloguing in Publication Data

Palda, Filip (K. Filip)
    Election finance regulation in Canada

    Includes bibliographical references.
    ISBN 0–88975–119–6

1. Campaign funds—Law and legislation—Canada.
   I. Fraser Institute (Vancouver, B.C.) II. Title.
   KE4646.P36 1991   342.71′078   C91–091531–8
   KF4920.P36 1991

Table of Contents

List of Tables

About the author

F ILIP PALDA RECEIVED HIS B.A. in 1983 and M.A. in 1984 in economics from Queen's University, Kingston. He continued his studies and in 1989 earned a PhD in economics from the University of Chicago. His dissertation, "Electoral Spending," was directed by thesis chairman Gary S. Becker. From 1989 to 1991, Dr. Palda was a professor of economics at the University of Ottawa. His specialties include public finance and public choice economics.

Acknowledgements

M Y THANKS GO TO PROFESSOR Thomas Borcherding of the Claremont Graduate School who made many valuable and detailed comments on an earlier draft, to Professor John Matsusaka of the University of Southern California School of Business for his comments and many discussions, and to Janice Coen of the University of Chicago for many proof readings and comments. I would also like to thank Jeff Moon and John Offenbeck of the Queen's Documents Library, and Andrew Currie of Queen's Computing Services for their expert help. Leslie Seidle of the Lortie Commission on Electoral Reform and Party Financing provided me with valuable information in the course of my research for the commission.

Dedication

The present work is dedicated to my mother.

Introduction and Overview

THE AIM OF THIS MONOGRAPH is to examine the consequences of regulating election campaign finances at the federal level in Canada. Such regulation usually comes in three forms: limits on election-time spending by candidates, parties, and private citizens; limits on contributions to politicians; and public funding of campaigns. Canada already has these regulations in some measure, but the debate continues on whether they need to be strengthened. This study describes the arguments in favour of regulation, and then suggests some dangers. A popular view is that spending and contribution limits, along with public subsidies, increase competition in elections and allow ordinary citizens to better participate, both as informed voters and as candidates. I suggest that these measures may actually hinder competition, entrench incumbents, and leave the electorate poorly informed of their choices.

The intent here is not to argue against the need for election finance regulation, but to bring attention to its hidden costs and to the narrow motives behind it. Most of what is known about the effects of regulation on public welfare comes from the study of economic markets where regulation often harms those it is meant to protect. For example, competition laws that break up large enterprises keep firms at small, inefficient levels of production, and lead to higher prices. Also, the almost complete blackout on advertising in the medical profession leaves patients ignorant of their best choices, and protects doctors from the consequences of having a bad record. To see if similar results carry over to election finance regulation, I borrow the economic notion of competition and apply it to politics. The analogy is not perfect but it helps to put together a coherent view of how campaign activities enable voters and candidates to exchange ideas and why it is important that they do so. The consequences of laws that interfere with the flow of election information can then be analyzed.

In the first chapter, I review the present laws governing spending, contributions, and subsidies in Canadian federal elections and describe the arguments commonly made in their favour. Chapter 2 asks whether spending limits really bring down the cost of elections as is claimed. In Chapter 3, I define political competition as a state in which incumbents cannot hold on to power by using the resources of the government to bias information about their performance. There is evidence that spending limits and franking privileges do this and that they serve to entrench incumbents. In this chapter I develop the theme, echoed through the remainder of the monograph, that politicians have a tendency to change the rules of the electoral game to their own advantage, and that this may explain the unanimity that "has become the tradition in the House of Commons when considering changes to the Canada Elections Act, which means refraining from all partisan debate."

Chapter 4 explains the many subtle ways in which political information travels between candidates and constituents. Polls, contributions, and "image" advertising are important sources of information which may suffer under regulation. Without this information, less informed voters have more trouble making an intelligent choice between candidates, and uninformed choice is bad because it does not punish misbehaviour by incumbents.

Chapter 5 asks why voter turnout is important and explains how campaign spending may promote turnout. I argue that voter turnout itself is of no value; instead what matters are the reasons people participate. If better information is the cause, then high turnout is a good sign. However, government programs which force people to participate are not desirable because they may disillusion the electorate and lead to bad political choices.

Chapter 6 is about the current movement in Canada to prevent advocacy groups and private citizens from joining election debates by advertising on behalf of a candidate or an issue. In the 1988 Canadian federal election these groups emerged as a major force in the free trade debate and much was said afterward of the need to keep them under control. The laws that are being proposed may benefit established parties and may be an important reason behind the creation of the 1990 Lortie Commission to study election finance regulation.

I describe the complicated issues of regulating campaign contributions in Chapter 7. Contributions may be used by special interests to buy political influence, but private citizens can also use contributions to impose discipline on candidates and to counter the work of narrowly-based but powerful lobbies.

Chapter 8 reviews current methods of public funding to campaigns and suggest that the formulas for allocating funds, and the complicated bureaucratic procedures to qualify for them, work against small parties. The chapter builds on the work of Paltiel (1980, 1984, 1985) who warned that campaign laws in western democracies are being rewritten to protect established parties against fringe parties and vocal citizens groups. Chapter 9 summarizes the findings.

Chapter 1

The Movement to Regulate Campaign Finances

Abstract

Election finance regulation at the federal level in Canada takes three forms: campaign spending limits; public subsidies to candidates and parties; and obligatory disclosure of campaign contributions. These measures are meant to serve the public by lowering the costs of elections, increasing competition, reducing corruption, and allowing ordinary citizens to better participate as voters and as candidates. This chapter outlines the law and describes the popular arguments made in its support.

Introduction

IN 1988, CANDIDATES AND PARTIES fought the Canadian federal election at a cost of $58 million. This was more than had ever been spent on an election in Canada. Public interest groups also joined the fray in 29 ridings, where according to one estimate they spent $18.5 million on behalf of candidates and causes (Filmore, 1989). Political observers noted these numbers and concluded that the spending limits in the Canada Elections Act were too low and too easy to circumvent and that the cost of elections had to be brought under control. In the mind of

Jean-Marc Hamel, former Chief Electoral Officer of Canada, parties had learned new ways of raising and spending money, and it was time to conduct a study like the 1966 Canadian Royal Committee on Election Reform (the Barbeau Committee) to guide major amendments to the law on election expenses (Hamel, 1989, p. 47).

Early in 1990, a new Royal Commission on Electoral Reform and Campaign Finance (also named the Lortie Commission, after its chair) was formed and toured Canada for three months to gather people's opinions and to suggest changes. Spending and contribution limits as well as government subsidies to politicians were an important concern, perhaps because the commissioners recognized that election money is such a large part of modern democracy, and because many private groups and politicians testified that such money needed to be better controlled in the interests of electoral competition.

In this chapter I suggest that the present movement for reform is grounded in the belief that spending regulation keeps down the cost of elections, contains corruption, and promotes competition between candidates. I outline Canadian campaign finance law and explain why people believe it needs to be strengthened. In subsequent chapters I explore some of the potential problems with these beliefs.

An outline of Canadian campaign finance law

In 1974 the federal government reformed election finance law by amending the Canada Elections Act; further amendments followed in 1977 and 1983 (Bill C-169).[1] The regulation sets the amount of money politicians can spend, the period in which they can advertise, and the types of expenditure allowed. The act also forbids private citizens and extraparliamentary groups from spending to promote or oppose the official contestants. Specifically:

1. Every candidate in a district may spend the same amount, but ceilings differ between districts according to the following formula:

---

1   Specifically, the government introduced Bill C-203 in 1974, which was passed into law as the Election Expenses Act.

- $1 for each of the first 15,000 names appearing on the preliminary list of electors;
- 50 cents for each name in excess of 15,000 but less than 25,000;
- 25 cents for each name in excess of 25,000;
- In vast districts, where fewer than 10 electors populate each square kilometre, an additional 15 cents to the limit for every square kilometre (up to a maximum of 25% of the ordinary limit) (*Canada Elections Act*, 1984, p. 154).

Parties may spend thirty cents for every name on the preliminary list of electors (s.13.2(1)) in a district where they present a candidate, and may deduct from their expenses anything that they donate to their candidates (s.13.2(1.1)). Expenditure limits are indexed to the Statistics Canada Consumer price index (base year 1981), and only apply during the election period; pre-writ spending is unregulated.

2. The law sets a ceiling on overall spending and in practice, though not in writ, restricts how money may be spent. Between them, the parties may buy no more than 6.5 hours of prime time advertisement from any broadcaster of radio or television (s.99.13). A party's fraction of these 6.5 hours is set in proportion to the votes it won in the last election.[2] No candidate may spend more than 1% of the limit to advertise his district nomination campaign (s.61.2(3a)).

3. The act defines expenditures as payments, liabilities (e.g. the use of an assembly hall on credit) and the commercial value of goods and services donated (e.g. corporate jets, advertising executives) other than volunteer labour (s.2.1). Some types of candidate spending do not come under the ceiling. The act exempts so-called personal expenses (s.61.1(3)), which are "any reasonable amount incurred by the candidate in respect of such travel, living and other related expenses as the Chief Electoral Officer may designate."(s.2.1) This is the only type of outlay the candidate himself can make. His agent must pay everything else.[3] The act

---

2   See Table 8.5 in Chapter 8 for a breakdown of time which each party was allowed to buy in the 1979, 1980, 1984, and 1988 elections.

3   The doctrine of 'agency,' which goes back to the Dominion Elections Act

also exempts the expenses of volunteers that the candidate takes on himself (e.g. food, lodgings, and transportation costs of door-to-door canvassers).

4. No one but a candidate, official agent, or representative of the candidate may incur election expenses (s.70.1(1)). This section came from several provisions in the notorious Bill C-169 which has been in limbo throughout Canada since Justice Medhurst of the Alberta Supreme Court declared it unconstitutional in his province (see Chapter 6).

5. No party or candidate may advertise on radio or television in either the first twenty-nine days or the last two days of the official campaign (s.13.7 and s.61.2(1))—federal campaigns usually last sixty days.

The act also reimburses parties and candidates in part for their expenditures, and gives generous tax allowances to small contributors (see Chapter 8). The names of people contributing more than $100 must be made available to the public (see Chapter 7).

Arguments behind the push for reform and trends in spending

The huge sums at play in the 1988 campaign, "rumours concerning certain members of Parliament from all parties" that have brought the enforcement sections of the Canada Elections Act into disrepute (Paltiel, 1988, p. 159) and citizens' group (also known as "third party") advertising, which "reared its head to an unprecedented extent in the 1988 election," (Hamel, 1989, p. 47) motivate the present movement for reform. What are the facts about federal campaign spending, and why do some people use them to argue for stricter limits?

Canada is a parliamentary democracy with three main parties: the Liberals, the Progressive Conservatives (also known as the P.C.s) and the New Democratic Party (the N.D.P.). When limits first took hold in 1979 none of these parties took much note. Senator Keith Davey, a senior

---

of 1874 but only came into force in 1974, applies to candidates but is aimed mainly at parties. Its purpose is to ensure that at least one person can be held to account for a party's breach of expenditure limits and fundraising practices.

fundraiser and advisor to the Liberals, observed that the 1979 limits for party spending were "a procedural rather than a real restraint" (Seidle and Paltiel, 1981, p. 253). In 1984, Bill C-169 raised the party spending ceilings to account for inflation and "experience accumulated in the previous decade" (Paltiel, 1988, p. 141). It removed the $2000 ceiling from candidates' personal expenses and broadened the definition of a large district.[4]

Table 1.1

Real Spending Limits (in 1989 $) for Parties and Candidates in the 1979, 1980, 1984 and 1988 Canadian Federal Elections

Year	Limits	
	Party (1000s of $)	Dollars per candidate per district
1979	$8,339	$51,402
1980	7,729[a]	47,227
1984	7,862	48,774
1988	8,406[b]	49,237

[a]The party limit on the N.D.P. in 1984 was $7,704 thousand (1989 values) because they did not present candidates in 2 of the 282 districts.

[b]The Liberal limit this year was $8,337 thousand (1989 values) perhaps because of the withdrawal of one Liberal candidate from his riding race.

Sources: *Report of the Chief Electoral Officer of Canada Concerning Election Expenses* for 1979, 1980, 1984, 1988. The Consumer Price Index was taken from the 1989 historical supplement to *The Canadian Economic Observer*.

---

4   The Chief Electoral Officer had argued in his 1983 Annual Report that "the provisions . . . which limit the amount a candidate may himself pay, to a maximum of $2,000, have caused significant difficulties" and that because party expenses have grown at the rate of inflation, in the 1984 election they would "find it difficult to campaign effectively within the spending limits established by the existing formula" (Hamel, 1983, p. 69).

Some idea of the relation of limits to campaign spending emerges from of Tables 1.1 to 1.4. Table 1.1 shows the real ceilings (in 1989 dollars) on parties and candidates for every election since 1979 (the first election to test the 1974 amendments). Despite the nominal increase in 1983, real ceilings on candidates were lower in 1984 than they had been in 1979 and were only marginally higher for parties. Table 1.2 shows that P.C. and N.D.P. candidates and parties have steadily neared their limits since 1979. Liberal candidates have actually receded from the limit, whereas the party has consistently spent around 90% of the maximum.

It appears that limits have imposed restraint upon politicians—as they were conceived to do—but these percentages do not capture the whole story. In 1984, Southam Press (owner of several major Canadian

Table 1.2

Percent of Spending Limits Attained by Parties and Candidates in the 1979, 1980, 1984, and 1988 Canadian Federal Elections

Year	Percent of Limit					
	Parties			**Candidates**		
	Liberal	P.C.	N.D.P.	Liberal	P.C.	N.D.P.[a]
1979	87.7%	86.2%	49.1%	79.8%	77.6%	34.4%
1980	84.6	96.9	68.1	77.5	72.4	38.3
1984	98.5	99.9	74.0	79.0	88.9	37.8
1988	85.7	98.9	88.1	69.9	52.8	85.8

[a]N.D.P. stands for the New Democratic Party. P.C. stands for the Progressive Conservatives.

Note: The percent of limits spent which the candidates attained are the average over all federal electoral districts, of which there were 282 in 1979, 1980, 1984 and 295 in 1988.

Sources: *Report of the Chief Electoral Officer of Canada Concerning Election Expenses* for 1979, 1980, 1984, 1988. The Consumer Price Index was taken from the 1989 historical supplement to *The Canadian Economic Observer*.

and British newspapers and magazines) found that 26 of the 28 MPs
they reviewed exploited slack rules in the "personal expenses" category
to legitimately spend, on average, $16,000 above their election expenses
limit (Stanbury, 1990). In 1979 and 1980, Liberal candidates spent closer
to their limits than either Conservatives or New Democrats, and declared a higher fraction of their spending as "personal" (see Table 1.3).

Table 1.3

Personal Expenses* of Candidates as a Percentage of Total Expenses in the 1979, 1980, 1984 and 1988 Canadian Federal Elections

Party	Election Year			
	1979	1980	1984	1988
Liberal	7.8%	8.9%	6.9%	5.1%
P.C.	7.5	8.7	7.9	5.9
N.D.P.	6.5	6.0	5.9	5.0

Note: These numbers are averages for each party's candidates over all
federal electoral districts.

* So called "Personal Expenses" are defined in the Canada Elections Act
(s.2.1) as "any reasonable amount incurred by the candidate in respect
of such travel, living and other related expenses as the Chief Electoral
Officer may designate." These expenses do not come under the official
spending limit.

Note: In 1979 and 1980 Liberals were closer to their limits than the P.C.s.
In those same years they declared a larger fraction of their spending as
personal. In 1984 and 1988 the analogous statement holds for the P.C.s.

Sources: *Report of the Chief Electoral Officer of Canada Concerning Election
Expenses* for 1979, 1980, 1984, 1988.

In 1984 and 1988, Conservative candidates were closest to the limit, and
it was their turn to declare the greater share of personal expenses.[5] Party

5   In the debate on the failed Bill C-79 (Canada's latest attempt at election
     reform) Liberal Member of Parliament Jacques Guibeault complained that,
     "anyone can exceed the imposed ceiling which is between $35,000 and

spending also soared high above the spirit of the law. Jerry Lampert, the former director of the P.C. Party, admitted that in the 1984 campaign, "the party used the computer data banks of its polling firm, Decima Research, to send letters to specially targeted voters in 30 ridings" at a cost of $20,000 *per riding*. Technically, none of this cost came under the official ceiling (Paltiel, 1988, p. 159). In addition, the Liberal and Conservative parties, who were especially close to the limits in 1984 and 1988, spent much more in the runup to those elections than they had in 1979 or 1980 (see Table 1.4). It appears as if they simply shifted their efforts to the inter-election period—on which the act is silent.

In frustration with such subtle manoeuvres, the Chief Electoral Officer reported that

Table 1.4

Party Campaign Expenses as a Percent of Total Party Expenses in Election Years

Year	Liberal	P.C.	N.D.P.
1979[a]	58.5%	43.0%	31.0%
1980[b]	51.0	47.0	34.0
1984[c]	34.0	23.5	38.0
1988[d]	40.0	27.3	32.0

[a]The 1979 election period was March 26 to May 22, 1979.

[b]The 1980 election period was December 14, 1979 to March 10, 1980.

[c]The 1984 election period was July 9 to September 4, 1984.

[d]The 1988 election period was October 1 to December 12, 1988.

Note: These numbers are averages for each party's candidates over all federal electoral districts.

Sources: *Report of the Chief Electoral Officer of Canada Concerning Election Expenses* for 1979, 1980, 1984, 1988.

$40,000 . . . which means that the spirit of the legislation is no longer respected and those who have lots of money can spend a great deal by using existing loopholes" (*House of Commons Debates*, 1988, p.13, 878).

the present definition of election expenses is so vague and imprecise that its application to various sections of the Act has become extremely difficult. Problems relating to pre-writ expenses, the principle of direct promotion of or opposition to a candidate or political party (third party advertising), the monies paid to agents and campaign workers, fund-raising, opinion surveys and the use of capital assets . . . must be looked at and clarified . . . in order that the system . . . not lend itself to variation of interpretation (Hamel, 1986, p. 10).

The Chief Electoral Officer also worried about enforcement of the law. The 1983 amendments contained in Bill C-169 struck away the 1974 requirement that an auditor verify that all party and candidate declarations comply with the Act. Due to a successful lobby by the accounting profession, auditors now need only decide whether returns by the politician to Elections Canada reflect transactions recorded by the candidate (Paltiel, 1988, p. 143). In other words, no receipts need be produced. This new slackening of vigilance has made it hard to prosecute overspenders.[6]

Candidates can get around some aspects of spending limits on their own, as the above examples illustrate, but they can also call on advocacy groups for help. Such groups played an important part in the 1988 federal election, promoting issues and candidates in the free trade debate. Their private campaigning stirred the fear that incumbents could avoid spending limits altogether by appealing to independent groups to spend on their behalf.

These trends and loopholes worry reformers who argue that regulation is in the public interest, and that more broadly defined limits, perhaps in combination with campaign subsidies and contribution and disclosure laws, would help achieve three objectives:

1. *Lower the costs of elections.* To many people elections seem to cost more than they did in the past. The sentiment is that political advertising is not productive—too much is spent on "image" advertising and too little on presenting the important political issues. A limit should be set to let candidates make their points without going overboard and dragging precious resources with

---

6   The Chief Electoral Officer's Statutory Reports after 1984 show fewer successful prosecutions for overspending (Hamel, 1989, pp. 41-42).

them. The question is how to "strike an equitable balance between limits so high they become meaningless and so low they ignore the fiscal reality of campaigning to the point where evasive tactics are required" (Ontario Commission on Election Finances, 1988, p. 14).

2. *Promote competition.* Spending limits combined with government subsidies to candidates are intended to make it possible for anyone to contest an election. By making seats in the Commons easier to contest, these measures should promote competition in elections. The Ontario Commission on Election Finance wrote that

> Financial inequality distorts the democratic process because it tends to impede marginally funded individuals from contesting an election. The expenditure limitations are, for the most part, aimed at advancing the goal of political equality between wealthy and less wealthy candidates, and between incumbents and challengers. (1988, p. 124)

John B. Anderson, a 1980 candidate for the American presidency, testified to Congress that campaign costs narrow "the pursuit of public office to those who possess great personal wealth or have access to large sums of money." Spending limits and subsides serve the public interest by stopping the "growing inequality in campaign finance and access to public office" (Abrams and Settle, 1978).

3. *Control contributions and corruption.* It was the Rivard affair of the late 1950s, suggestions that the underworld was funding politicians, and the example of the corrupt Duplessis government in Quebec that inspired the Barbeau Commission to endorse spending limits in its 1966 report (Seidle and Paltiel, 1981, pp. 229-230). In the United States, Walter Mondale maintained that "the evidence in the Watergate hearings shows it is now standard practice in politics to put Government . . . up for sale to the highest bidder" (Abrams and Settle, 1978). Democrats of like mind used the Watergate scandal to regulate spending by presidential candidates. The idea in both countries was that if candidates spent less, they would accept less from large contributors. Government subsidies to candidates, tax allowances for small contributors,

laws that oblige large donors names to be made public, are also
suggested as a means to lessen the influence of large contributors.

Conclusion

The list of reasons for regulation presented here is not comprehensive,
but it outlines the main worries of those who favour reform. Many of
these reasons are powerful and convincing, but because so much is at
stake, caution is advised in revising current election law. Where do these
arguments fall short and what are the dangers and costs of restricting
spending and contributions, and subsidizing campaigns? The remainder of this monograph is devoted to investigating these questions.

Chapter 2

Trends in Election Costs

Abstract

Rising advertising fees are often blamed for the large sums spent in elections; spending limits are one proposed means of keeping down costs. However, the amount spent on an election is not a useful measure of cost. The dollar price of informing a given number of voters about a political platform is a better cost index because it gives an idea of the productivity of campaign spending. There are indications that costs, defined in this manner, have been falling as advertising technology has improved. There is also reason to believe that the complicated rules surrounding spending limits can increase these costs.

Introduction

COSTS HAVE A BAD NAME in elections and attract the attention of some reformers who consider parts of campaign spending wasteful and in need of control. They feel that too much is spent on "hype" and too little on the important issues. Spending limits are seen as a way of obliging politicians to make their case to the public succinctly and to refrain from unproductive clashes of personality and from the senseless, aggrandizing promotion of their "image." Here I argue that if, on the contrary, campaign spending is seen as a useful activity, then *the amount spent on a campaign* is a misleading measure of cost. The *cost of informing a given number of voters* is more meaningful because it reflects how productive campaign spending is.

I review trends in election spending in the Canada, Great Britain, and the U.S., and suggest that because of improvements in advertising technology, the price of informing voters has fallen. Even though advertisements cost more today, they reach greater numbers of people, so that the price of informing any given voter may actually be lower than in the past. The complicated rules that surround spending limits may indeed reduce what is spent on a campaign, but they may also interfere with the ability of candidates to communicate with voters, which means that a dollar's worth of advertising influences fewer people than it might were it unregulated. Thus, spending regulation may increase the costs of informing voters even though the amount spent on campaign falls.

Do elections today really cost more than in the past?

Let us look at the evidence for a change in campaign costs. Perhaps the first detailed study of long-term trends in election campaign costs was made by Abrams and Settle (1978). They analyzed American presidential elections in an era before campaign regulation (1900-1972) and found no sign that as a group, candidates were spending more (see Table 2.1). *Nominal* spending—spending not adjusted for the cost of living—had risen, of course, but in real terms, the 1928 and 1936 campaigns were more expensive than any until 1972. They also found that real spending *per adult* showed no trend whatsoever, and that spending as a fraction of GNP had fallen steadily.[1] In Britain's case, Pinto-Duschinsky (1981) found no evidence of rising costs in Parliamentary elections. Central party spending was much lower in 1979 than in 1964 and "Indeed,

---

1   Other researchers (Campaign Finance Study Group, 1979, Ch. 1, p. 17) added that spending was really very low because electoral politics are in competition with corporate advertising for the attention of Americans. In the 1976 elections, all candidates for federal office spent in sum $212 million on campaign advertising, while private industry spent $33.6 billion (150 times the sum of campaign budgets) on commercial advertising.

Table 2.1

Year	Millions Spent ($)	Cents spent per adult (¢)	(Total Spending / GNP) x 1000
1900	$14.15	33.60	0.12
1904	10.87	23.30	0.08
1908	8.46	16.60	0.06
1912	7.39	13.40	0.04
1916	12.80	21.80	0.06
1920	10.34	16.50	0.05
1924	12.15	18.00	0.05
1928	27.80	38.30	0.10
1932	18.38	23.80	0.09
1936	40.45	49.40	0.14
1940	18.40	21.30	0.05
1944	—	—	—
1948	7.02	7.20	0.01
1952	15.72	15.80	0.03
1956	17.02	16.40	0.03
1960	25.13	23.10	0.03
1964	31.33	27.50	0.04
1968	43.10	36.00	0.04
1972	74.00	55.60	0.06
1976	28.83	19.30	0.02
1980	29.68	23.90	0.02

U.S. Presidential Campaign Spending (in 1972 $)[a]

[a] Adapted and updated from Abrams and Settle, 1978.

despite comments about the Conservative's use of 'modern' media techniques, the party spent no more, in real terms, on centrally-funded publicity than it had half a century earlier in 1929" (p. 236). This is a significant observation, because parties, rather than individual candidates, do most of the spending in British elections.

Data for the Canadian case are unavailable before 1974, but after then, the Abrams-Settle measurements can be made for Canada.

Table 2.2

Three Measures of the Cost of Campaigning for Parties and Candidates in Canadian Federal Elections (in 1989 $)

Sum over Parties

Year	Real Spending (1000s $)	Real Spending per adult ($)	(Spending / GDP) x 1000
1979	$18,614	$1.22	0.065
1980	19,250	1.24	0.066
1984	21,499	1.26	0.069
1988	22,916	1.18	0.062

Sum over Candidates in Average District

Year	Real Spending (1000s $)	Real Spending per adult ($)	(Spending / GDP) x 1000
1979	$98.58	$1.82	0.097[a]
1980	86.41	1.58	0.083
1984	102.19	1.70	0.093
1988	102.68	1.56	0.083

[a]This number is average district spending divided by average district GDP, which I roughly calculated as GDP / # of districts.

Note: All figures are in 1989 dollars (calculated with the Consumer Price Index). The amounts minor parties spent is not included.

Sources: *Report of the Chief Electoral Officer of Canada Concerning Election Expenses* for 1979, 1980, 1984, 1988. Population calculated from Tables 2.11 and 2.12 of the 1990 *Canada Yearbook*. CPI and GDP taken from the 1990 historical supplement to the *Canadian Economic Observer*.

Table 2.2 shows similar calculations for the Canadian federal elections of 1979, 1980, 1984, and 1988, with results similar to the U.S. presidential elections. Despite a steady rise in real limits since 1980, real per capita spending, and spending as a fraction of gross domestic product, has fallen. These figures do not tell the whole story though, because parties also spend between elections. Table 2.3 shows that real spending by all parties between elections (an unregulated period) rose dramatically in real terms.

A useful definition of cost

The U.S., British and Canadian cases suggest that there is nothing that obliges campaign costs to rise steadily over time, and that cost calculations depend on the measure of cost adopted (nominal, real, real per capita, spending per dollar of gross domestic product). Nevertheless, the rising cost of elections seems to be an article of faith with many policymakers, and this faith is often accompanied by the doctrine that high costs are bad and wasteful. In 1966 the Barbeau Committee on Election Expenses called for shorter campaigns and for a ban on advertising except during the last four weeks before polling day, in order to reduce campaign costs. Recently the Ontario Commission on Election Finances (1988) has restated the widespread belief that limits can contain the alleged surge in the cost of campaigns.

A different, and perhaps surprising, proposition which has received less attention is that high election costs are not necessarily bad and that low election costs are not necessarily good. High costs may signal that advertising and other campaign activities are priced in the market to reflect the value candidates place upon them. Candidates place a high value on advertising if it is an effective way of getting information to voters. Advertising is also of value to voters because it lowers their costs of collecting information about the issues and the candidates, making it easier for them to choose intelligently. Low costs that result from official spending limits may be bad if, as a result, voters are deprived of information. Paradoxically, spending limits, in their many variations and their complicated administration, may actually increase the costs of transmitting information between candidates and voters. This is not to say that more money will be spent under limits, but that restricted spending may be of less value to the electorate because spending

Table 2.3

Real Spending by Parties (in 1000s of 1989 $)

Non-Election Periods

Year	Liberal	P.C.	N.D.P.	Total Spent
1974	$5,614[a]	$4,567	$3,632[d]	—
1975	—[b]	2,295[c]	6,633.7	—
1976	12,150[b]	8,395	5,644	—
1977	9,311	9,414	6,905	$25,630
1978	10,795	11,177	7,180	29,152
1979	5,185	9,511	8,753	23,449
1980	9,788	8,362	10,178	28,338
1981	7,725	11,388	9,801	28,915
1982	7,491	11,613	9,318	28,422
1983	8,087	13,319	10,319	31,726
1984	14,815	25,653	9,145	49,613
1985	9,674	13,835	13,143	36,651
1986	12,735	16,128	17,322	46,184
1987	10,133	14,739	15,310	40,182
1988	10,686	22,183	15,681	48,547

Campaign Spending

Year	Liberal	P.C.	N.D.P.	Total Spent
1979	$7,322	$7,195	$4,098	$18,614
1980	6,533	7,486	5,242	19,260
1984	7,770	7,888	5,841	21,499
1988	7,183	8,319	7,415	22,916

[a]The Liberals only submitted a 12 month report for the period August 1, 1974 to July 31, 1975.
[b]The Liberals only submitted a 17 month report from August 1, 1975 to December 31, 1976.
[c]The Conservatives only submitted a 5 month report from August 1, 1975 to December 31, 1975.
[d]The New Democrats only submitted a 5 month report from August 1, 1974 to December 31, 1974.

Note: All numbers are in 1989 dollars. All reports were annual, except for the ones listed in a–d above.
Sources: *Report of the Chief Electoral Officer of Canada Concerning Election Expenses* for 1979, 1980, 1984, 1988.

regulation often makes it hard for candidates to get their messages across efficiently.

Because there are many ways to define cost, it is important that the definition be precise because cost is easily confused with the final amount spent on a campaign. In turn, this confusion can mislead policy analysis. Cost is the monetary and material expense of achieving a certain result. In the case of an election the result in question is communication with the public. Once a standard of communication (candidate recall after five days, thousands of households reached, etc.) is chosen, it becomes possible to speak of the per-unit cost of campaigning: how many dollars the candidate must spend to reach a given number of people. If unit costs rise, the total spent on a campaign may rise. Conversely, if the candidate's desire to reach constituents shrinks rapidly in reaction to higher unit costs, the total spent on the campaign may fall. It is also possible for unit costs to fall, and the amount spent on a campaign to rise. Unit costs and total costs are separate quantities with different meanings.

The effect of spending regulations on cost

To see how regulation can increase unit cost, consider the section of the Canada Elections Act that limits the parties together to 6.5 hours of prime-time advertising in the 29 days before the election campaign. Parties try to spend their money on activities in combinations that produce effective results. A regulation that restricts the use of one activity, such as advertising, tampers with this "optimal input mix" and raises the costs of reaching any given number of voters.[2] Costs may have also risen due to successive amendments to the act (1977, 1983) which have substantially increased the paperwork that is required to run a party and qualify for reimbursements (Paltiel, 1989). It is difficult to gather evidence for the changes in costs, or to prove conclusively the

---

2   A standard result of economic theory is that a firm's costs will be higher if it cannot vary an input, as it might not be able to in the short run. Costs are higher in the short run than in the long run, when all inputs are variable and the firm has freedom to arrange its production as it wishes.

cause of the change, but some evidence comes from America where according to a group of Harvard researchers,

> the Federal Election Campaign Act has itself increased the costs of election campaigning in two ways. Costs of compliance with the Act divert scarce resources from activities which involve communications with voters. And, more significantly, in strictly limiting the amounts of money that individuals can contribute to campaigns, the Act has unintentionally increased the costs of raising campaign funds. (Campaign Finance Study Group, 1979, Ch. 1, p. 17)

Unit costs rose in the U.S. because of the administrative burden of the regulation, but also because the regulation made it more costly to solicit funds from individuals. The U.S. law limited presidential spending and placed an onerous administrative burden on Congressional candidates. Soon after its passage, the cost of Congressional campaigns exploded. In a report to Congress, the Campaign Finance Study Group (1978 , Ch.1, p. 14) wrote that "The available data demonstrate that the costs of campaigning have increased markedly since 1972. Between 1972 and 1978 the amount of money raised (and spent) by Congressional candidates increased by 34% over and above the rise in the consumer price index." Many forces have contributed to this increase in costs, including a desire by candidates to spend more, but the Campaign Finance Study Group suggested that complicated campaign laws may also have been partly responsible.

Spending regulation can also increase unit costs by forcing a party to shift its spending to the pre-campaign period—during which advertising is not nearly as effective as it is during the campaign, when the public is more attentive. For Canada, the evidence is indirect, but Table 2.3 suggests that parties have been shifting spending to the period between campaigns. Unless this shift happened because of technological reasons that made advertising or organizing more productive in the interim, there is reason to suspect that parties have been forced to behave inefficiently as a result of spending limits.

It is important to caution that even though Table 2.3 shows that each party is spending more, this may have nothing to do with changes in unit costs. This is why I call the evidence indirect. The ambiguity arises because current theoretical research has not yet settled whether more actually gets spent when unit costs change. If all candidates are equally matched, an increase in the costs of informing voters may not necessarily lead to more spending. The situation can be compared to a tennis match in which the sun emerges from the clouds to distract both players. If both players are equally affected, nothing has really changed, and there is no reason for them to exert more or less effort. If, however, one of the players performs better in the sun, he may choose to exert himself more and his opponent may choose a lower level of effort. What happens to the overall level of effort (or campaign spending, in the case of an election) is not clear.[3] In other words, the amount spent depends on more than just unit costs. It also depends on how much the candidates *wish* to spend.

Cost increases due to higher advertising prices

An increase in *costs* due to regulation is not the same as a rise in the *price* of advertising. In the U.S. the nominal price of prime time advertisement rose by 64% between 1972 and 1976 (Campaign Finance Study Group, Ch. 1, p. 15) and the trend continues to this day, as those who follow the Superbowl and its many specialized statistics will recognize. However, commentators point out that more and more people watch the Superbowl and that the ads that accompany it are better researched and more effective than they used to be. Advertising costs more because it is more productive, and since it is more productive, the unit cost of reaching any given viewer may have fallen.[4]

There is reason to believe that the same is true of political advertising, and that a dollar today allows candidates to reach more voters than in the past, even though the price of advertising has risen. Politicians spend a large part of their budgets to convince voters (the other part goes to fund-raising). To do this, they advertise in the press and on

---

3   See Rosen, 1986 for a good discussion of "Tournament Theory," which examines how the efforts of contestants in win-lose contests varies with the size of the prize and the skill of the players.

4   The cost of reaching an extra viewer is the cost of, say, a minute of advertising, divided by the productivity of that advertisement. Hence, advertising may be an inexpensive way of reaching large numbers of people even though the costs per minute appear large.

television, and employ professional staff who plan their schedules, mobilize volunteers, flush out "photo-opportunities," and steer them from gaffes.[5] The campaign organizer of today is much better at his job than was his counterpart fifty years ago and works with better tools. Modern election television commercials benefit from decades of research in psychology and marketing.[6] They get their point across more efficiently and it is remembered longer than in the past.[7] In addition, audiences are more educated today which means that more information can be packed into messages of any given length.

Conclusion

The amount spent on a campaign is not a figure which by itself should give cause for concern. Regulations aimed at controlling costs may actually do the reverse and deprive voters of valuable information. The next three chapters further explore the value of information to voters.

---

5   The Trudeau campaign of 1980 is an exception. Trudeau's party deemed him such a liability that they hid him from view in the hope that voters would not notice him. For example, he refused to appear in a televised all-candidate debate.

6   Margaret Thatcher's 1979 electoral blitzkrieg was planned in part by the high-tech British advertising firm of Saatchi and Saatchi.

7   To get a better feel for the fall in the cost of informing people, consider that in ancient Sumer, Gudea, the ruler of Lagash, distributed his effigy, expensively carved in diorite, to hundreds of public squares to advertise his reign. Today, a two-page spread in the *Iraqi Herald* would do the trick.

Chapter 3

Should Campaign Spending be Regulated?

Abstract

Restrictions on campaign spending are supposed to promote electoral competition and to work in the public interest, but they may in fact allow incumbents to hold on to office and may harm the public. Incumbents favour limits because on average, challengers get more return for the dollars they spend in election campaigns. Limits help incumbents preserve the vote advantage they built while promoting themselves between elections with government resources. The resulting stability makes them less sensitive to the needs of constituents.

Introduction

IT IS WIDELY HELD THAT campaign spending must be controlled in order to protect competition in elections. In this chapter I suggest that constituents may be better served by free races in which candidates can spend as much as they wish. At the heart of this argument is the idea that money enables valuable information to flow between candidates and constituents. Candidates commission polls to discover what constituents want, adjust their platforms accordingly, and then advertise their platforms. Advertising lowers the cost to voters of making an intelligent choice. Political competition flourishes when challengers can advertise mistakes or misdeeds that incumbents have made in office. A competitive political system is one in which the threat of being unseated is great enough to keep the ruler honest and attentive to the needs of constituents. Campaign spending maintains this threat. For this reason, when one side manages to stifle the other, as it might with a spending limit, competition suffers and electorates remain poorly informed of their options.

The empirical evidence for the claim that spending regulations hurt competition comes from American and Canadian studies (see Jacobson, 1978, 1985; Palda and Palda, 1985, among others) out of which two findings repeatedly emerge:

1. Incumbents start their races with a large block of voters already favourably disposed to them.
2. Incumbents gain fewer votes from advertising than challengers do.

A spending limit keeps down challenger spending, which, as will be explained later, is more potent, and in so doing preserves the incumbent's block of supporters. At the same time, the limit reduces the incumbent's cost of winning. Put differently, with less money to spend, challengers will have trouble becoming well known and criticizing incumbents. Incumbents will feel safer; they will pay less attention to their duties and may abuse their privileges at the expense of taxpayers. In this sense limits reduce competition.

Spending limits, however, are only a part of our complicated and subtle spending law. The Canada Elections Act restricts not only the total that may be spent but also the types of expenditure, and the period in which spending can be done. These aspects may favour one party over another, and one candidate over another. In the last part of the chapter, I explain how these adjuncts to basic limits tilt the campaign playing field and thus how they change political competition.

In whose interest are spending limits?

Spending limits are supposed to promote competition in elections by ensuring that the richest candidates do not spend their way into office. It is believed that they work in the public interest by allowing any citizen with good ideas to run for election without fear of losing to a wealthy opponent. Abrams and Settle (1978) have criticized this public interest view on grounds that regulations which appear to protect one group (voters) may actually be written for the benefit of different group (politicians):

> Rational, self-interested individuals, groups, or industries seek regulation as a means of serving their own private interests. . . . When regulation has the potential for directly affecting the legislators themselves (e.g. political campaign regulations), the economic approach suggests that the regulation would be designed to serve the legislators' interest rather than some vaguely defined "public interest."

The economic approach to which they refer is due to Stigler who argued that "every industry or occupation that has enough political power to utilize the state will seek to control entry" (Stigler, 1971). In economic markets, existing firms can charge consumers higher prices if they restrict the entry of competitors. When applied to political markets, this approach reveals that, contrary to popular opinion, spending limits make it hard to enter politics. Legislators are tempted to exploit popular fears about the use of money in elections to pass laws that make it hard for challengers to compete; laws which may have unpleasant consequences for the people whom on the surface they were meant to protect. Under certain circumstances—which seem to prevail in democratic elections—limits benefit incumbents by increasing their vote margins and consequently their hold on power. This extra power can (in ways to be elaborated) make it easier for incumbents to act in their own narrow interests to the detriment of the majority. Incumbents as a whole may profit from simple limits but the possibilities do not end here. When certain categories of spending, such as volunteer labour, are exempt, incumbents from the party which relies most on volunteers will profit the most in votes. The details of limits and allied regulation governing how campaign resources may and may not be used affects competition as much as the simple limits themselves do.

Political competition

Political competition is an admired concept but exactly what it means is a subject of debate. It is widely held that a political system is compet-

itive if incumbents do not stay long in power and that it lacks competition if candidates win by wide margins. For example, Ferejohn (1977)
defined a competitive seat as one in which the margin of victory does
not exceed 20%. Fears about unbeatable incumbents seem to be stronger
in the U.S. than in Canada because levels and trends in reelection differ
between the two countries. Garand and Gross (1983) found that in
Congressional races, incumbents' margins of victory grew in the years
between 1896 and 1966, and that since then winners showed a mild
tendency to win by bigger margins. Canada, on the other hand, has had
a higher rate of incumbent turnover on average over the past thirty years
(see Table 3.1) and there is no indication of a trend toward longer terms
(see Krashinsky and Milne, 1985).

It is tempting to conclude from these numbers that public office in
Canada is more open to newcomers and that this prevents the accumu-

Table 3.1

Percentage of Incumbent Legislators who Sought Re-election and were Re-elected: House of Commons and U.S. House of Representatives

Election Pair	Country	
	Canada	U.S.
1957-58	59	92
1958-62	55	68
1962-63	79	90
1963-65	76	82
1965-68	55	73
1968-72	58	66
1972-74	79	81
1974-79	58	59
1979-80	81	81

Note: "Election Pair" shows the date of adjacent elections. The U.S.
figures are adjusted to match the period between Canadian elections.
Source: Adapted from Thompson and Stanbury, 1984.

lation and abuse of power in the hands of a few long-term political players. The link between turnover and power, however, is not clear and a closer look at this particular question can give a feel of the broader concept of political competition. Incumbents may be reelected more often than challengers simply because they are better at their jobs and voters are happy with things as they are. In economic markets, competition is seldom measured by how long the main producers have been around or by the longevity of managers and entrepreneurs. Instead, competition is thought to depend on how easily one competitor can contest the actions of another. More precisely, economic competition is a state in which producers are not able to alter conditions in the market to earn profit above the rewards due their natural abilities. A monopoly is not competitive because it earns "abnormal" profits by keeping potential rivals out, usually with the help of government (the Ontario Milk Marketing Board, for instance, is a monopoly which the government has granted to a few special producers). Competition is likely to reign in markets where each producer can contest the other's price. It is not necessary that there be many producers—even one may do—or that new producers enter the market regularly. All that is required is for each to know that if he attempts to raise his price for abnormal profit at the consumer's expense, another producer will appear to contest him with a lower price.

The private market is an appealing and useful analogy for elections; it leads to the following definition:

> In an ideal democracy competition is free in the sense that no appreciable costs or artificial barriers prevent an individual from running for office and from putting a platform before the electorate (Becker, 1958).

Politicians are similar to producers. They lure customers (voters) with the promise of efficient, honest and intelligent service in office. In return, they get prestige and the control of government resources. A dissatisfied majority of customer-voters can end the contract by voting the incumbent out of office. They might do so because he has proven himself corrupt, or lazy and inefficient: "If one party becomes extortionate (or badly mistaken in its reading of effective desires), it is possible to elect another party which will provide the governmental services at a price more closely proportioned to the costs of the party" (Stigler,

1971). Competition suffers when an incumbent can keep challengers in check with methods that do not rely on the support of voters. Protected by "artificial barriers" the politician can pay himself an abnormal sum (a sum above the "costs of the party") from his clients' (the public) purse. For example, the political machines of Daley in Chicago and Duplessis in Quebec tampered with ballots to stifle competition. These regimes, which were noted for their exceptionally high level of corruption and their disregard for public welfare, endured behind strong political barriers.[1]

Taking this view, the length of the term itself is not a good index of competition, and must be seen in context. High turnover may be due to some intrinsic randomness in the preferences of the electorate and may have little to do with the politician's performance. It is not length of term which determines competition but whether politicians lose their jobs for being inattentive to the electorate. The same length of term can be a sign of two very different forces at play. Franklin Roosevelt and Adolf Hitler held office for nearly the same time but there is no comparison between the way the two regimes performed. If an incumbent can raise barriers to challengers, as Hitler did with enormous talent, he will stay in office longer and competition will suffer. Incumbents who satisfy the needs of the electorate and respond to their demands, as Roosevelt did, will also keep office but with very different results. The comparison between German Nazism and American democracy may appear extreme but it brings out the point that one cannot judge a regime on the basis of simple indices such as turnover. Attention should go to the institutions that govern the flow of money in elections. The following sections discuss why spending limits, the use of government resources by incumbents for self-promotion, and short elections may act as barriers to entry.

---

1   Stigler (1971) noted that the market analogy is not perfect because the channels of political decision making are "gross or filtered or noisy" in the sense that in politics many people must decide at once, making voting on specific issues very costly and forcing voters to "eschew direct expressions of marginal changes in preferences," but that the analogy is close enough to conclude that "if a political party has monopoly control over the governmental machine, one might expect that it could collect most of the benefits of regulation for itself."

Discussion of other barriers such as campaign subsidies is left to Chapter 8.

A model of the election campaign

To see why spending regulation might deter potential candidates from entering an election race, it helps to have a model that explains how candidates get their message across and why this promotes competition. It is generally agreed that candidates win support by spending money (Palda, 1973, 1975). A candidate spends money on polls to learn what people want. He chooses which of his ideas and personal qualities will appeal to the majority and then advertises them. His information will reach part of the constituency and will put him in a good light in the eyes of some. On polling day, if they remember, he may get their support. At worst, voters may find nothing of interest in the message and opinions will not change.

The more a candidate spends, the more people he reaches. He will reinforce his message with some who have already heard it and he will also reach new ears. However, each extra dollar brings less support than the previous one. The "marginal" (extra) product of spending falls because as more is spent the proportion of old ears to new ears rises. For example, suppose a person gets nothing from hearing the message a second time. Then as a candidate spends more he reaches more people that he has already informed and this does him no good. In the limit, everyone is an old ear and the candidate might as well not advertise.[2] Figure 1.1 illustrates this idea. Votes rise as spending increases but by less with each extra dollar, which is why the curve becomes less steep.

Why limits restrict competition

How well money transmits information and sways voters depends on the spender and the context. Is the candidate female, an incumbent, a good speaker? Is the constituency wealthy, educated, religious? A female candidate may spend a fortune in a traditional riding and get nowhere, or might spend little in a liberal-minded riding and do quite

---

2   I am discussing so-called positive advertising, but the same holds true for ads that smear an opponent.

Votes

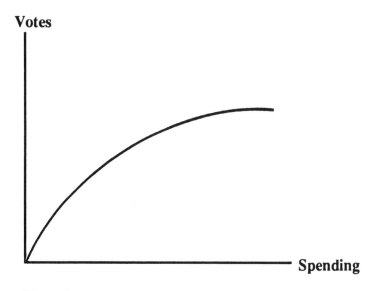

Figure 1

Campaign spending has a diminishing effect on a candidate's votes. More spending (all else constant) increases votes, but at a falling rate. This is why the curve relating votes to spending has a positive but diminishing slope.

well. In other words, money alone does not determine election outcomes; there are many other forces that may interact subtly with spending. In search of these interactions, dozens of studies (see Johnston, 1987, for a bibliography) have isolated the effects of spending, candidate traits, and district features on votes. Two findings emerge repeatedly from American and Canadian studies:

1. *Challengers gain more votes for every dollar they spend than incumbents do.* Jacobson (1979b) found that in 1974 House elections, challengers gained on average 12.1% of the vote for every $10,000 they spent, whereas incumbents only gained 2.8%. Jacobson used a technique known as "regression" which accounts for the possibility that as anticipated votes rise due to spending, contributions

and hence spending will rise and that this brings more votes, which brings more contributions, and so on.[3] Palda and Palda (1985) found that challenger spending in Ontario federal ridings in 1979 brought 0.62 votes for every dollar, while first-term incumbents only got 0.36 extra votes and higher-term incumbents received 0.29 extra votes.

2 *Incumbents start each race with a greater block of initial voter support than challengers do.* Palda and Palda (1985) found that being a first term incumbent at the constituency level in the 1979 Canadian Federal Elections was worth an extra 8,100 votes. Higher term incumbents could expect 12,200 extra votes at the outset.

Incumbent spending between elections may explain these findings. Between elections incumbents promote themselves ceaselessly at government expense. With their paid office staff, franking, and travel privileges they advertise, and meet voters. By the next election they will already have been campaigning for years, building the large initial block of supporters of the type documented by Jacobson (1978). In the process they will have exhausted the large initial returns to spending. This fits the common finding that incumbents get less response per dollar spent in campaigns. Seen from a different perspective, challengers come to the race able to reap a larger crop of "new ears" which is why they gain more from campaigning than do incumbents. In Jacobson's words, "Campaign money is most important to nonincumbent candidates. If electoral competition is valued, then it is clear that too little, not too much money has been spent on most Congressional campaigns." (Jacobson, 1979a, Ch. 2, p. 37). An independent survey of Congressional candidates seems to support his results: "In all this [the survey] it is the malaise of competitive challengers that is most apparent, and most troubling for those who want to promote electoral rivalry. They are the ones (by a

---

3   In another study, Jacobson (1978) also found that voters are more likely to remember a challenger's message than an incumbent's message. He may have found this result because the people he interviewed were "old ears," and were not likely to be changed by extra incumbent spending. He interpreted this to mean that such people were less likely to remember incumbents. My model indicates, rather, that such people were less susceptible to the incumbent's message.

margin of 4 to 1 [in the survey]) who say that additional funds would have made a difference in their campaigns" (Orren, 1979, Ch. 3, p. 20).

Spending limits as barriers

Spending limits might help incumbents at the polls if, as argued above, they get less response per dollar spent and start the race with a large initial block of support. A spending limit would add votes to this block while at the same time lowering the amount the incumbent had to pay for a victory! To see this better, consider how the vote margins of challengers and incumbents would have differed in the 1979 Canadian contest had expenditure ceilings been lower than the average of $27,487. As mentioned earlier, Palda and Palda (1985) found that challengers received 0.62 votes for every dollar they spent, holding all else constant, and that first and second term incumbents received 0.36 and 0.29 votes respectively. This means that a binding drop of, say, $1000 in permissible expenditures would have cost a challenger fighting a battle with a first term incumbent 260 votes (0.62-0.36=0.26 multiplied by 1000), and 330 votes (0.62-0.29=0.33 multiplied by 1000) in a contest to a second term incumbent.[4] At a ceiling of zero, incumbents would have maximized their margins and minimized their costs. Limits are barriers to entry because they may it more difficult for challengers to win. Competition suffers because limits make it difficult for challengers to criticize incumbents and advertise possibly more attractive platforms and alternatives to the electorate.[5]

---

4   What one candidate loses in votes, the other gains. Thus the 0.36 votes first term incumbents receive for every dollar comes at the expense of challengers. The net effect on challenger votes of a reduction in all candidates' spending will be (0.62 - 0.36) x 1000.

5   Limits may not hinder competition if they bind only the official contestants because challenging candidates can get around them by finding groups of people to campaign on their behalf. For example, a Christian television network invites pro-life candidates to make their case on the air without charge; or an ecology group denounces the way the governing party handled an oil spill on a fragile coast. Dodges like these taught regulators that they must limit what private individuals and groups can spend if they want expenditure law to work. Chapter 6 looks at so-called third-party spending restrictions in detail.

Under certain circumstances, this reasoning must be refined to include political contributions. Incumbents seem better able to raise money than challengers (Stanbury, 1986) which means that a spending limit would take away this particular advantage. Whether incumbents still benefit from spending limits depends on their ability to raise money and on the power of challenger spending. If incumbents can raise twice as much as challengers but challenger spending is four times as potent, limits benefit incumbents. Incumbents will like limits even if they can raise twice as much but challenger spending is only twice as potent; vote margins will not be affected but incumbents will spend less. At lower levels of challenger productivity, however, incumbents will receive higher vote margins in a free spending race. Strangely, if a limit is set, incumbents will favour a low one. The reason for this paradox is that once limits bind both candidates neither has an advantage in money raising ability. All that remains is the effect on votes from lowering spending and, as illustrated earlier, this favours incumbents. Incumbents may prefer no limits to limits, but if limits are applied they will want them to be low.

Franking privileges as barriers

Spending limits are not the only barriers to entry. Incumbents enjoy government-supplied resources that they use to win reelection. Franking privileges, office staff, and paid travel come first to mind but the treasury can be tapped in other ways. Shortly before an election the reigning government may start an official campaign to "inform" citizens of what is being done perhaps for the elderly or for economic development or by some Royal Commission. The Liberal government followed this course in the 1984 campaign when it placed $21 million of official advertisements—about three times its normal summer advertising—mainly with agencies that were active in promoting the party's campaign (Paltiel, 1988, p. 158).

The value of government resources used by incumbents is difficult to estimate, but Welch (1981) surmised for Congress that in two years an incumbent spends several hundred thousand dollars in public funds for his office staff and franked mailings and that some, if not all, of these expenditures are directed to his reelection. Carter and Racine (1990) found that between elections incumbents enjoyed, on average, campaign expenditures of $0.55 per capita or, a little over 200,000 1982 American dollars. In work for the Lortie Commission on Election Financing, Palda (1990) found that in 1984 Canadian incumbents enjoyed an advantage of $51,000. By 1988, this advantage had risen to $82,000. These privileges explain in part why incumbents expect a solid block of votes even before the campaign has started. Damage to competition would be smaller if the privileges were brought under a campaign spending ceiling but this is a difficult prescription to follow because the value of government resources is hard to estimate and it is not clear what fraction goes to the ordinary business of governing and what fraction goes to self-promotion between campaigns. The best solution would be instead to simply let campaign spending go unregulated.

Short elections as barriers

In Canada, challengers have sixty days (the average length of federal elections) to become known to their constituency. Short campaigns can harm challengers by not giving them enough time to use their resources efficiently. Campaigns are the best time to advertise because voters are in a high state of awareness—government programs advise the electorate that a race is on, and politics is in the news. The campaign atmosphere complements efforts by politicians to get attention. Challengers benefit most from this attention because initially few people know what they stand for. A short election cuts this time of high excitement during which challengers can use their money to best effect. They can, of course, advertise before the election, but it is harder to inform voters then because there are no free inputs, such as newscasts, to draw added attention to their political advertising. Incumbents also inform fewer people in short elections, but they do not suffer as much because so many already know them. The final effect of shortening the campaign could be to lower the marginal product of challenger spending on challenger votes, to the advantage of the incumbent.

Criticisms of the Incumbent Interest
View of Regulation

I have argued that spending limits are good for incumbents, but if this is true, why did Parliament raise limits and index them to inflation in

1983? Why do candidates seem to spend on average significantly less than the law permits? It is quite possible that, contrary to the preceding arguments, incumbents do not profit from limits but pass legislation to that effect to satisfy the public. Testimony to the Lortie Commission suggests that many Canadians think that the amount of money spent in elections is out of control. Incumbents may have voted for the 1974 limits to cool public anger, while keeping them high enough to present nothing more than a procedural restraint. They may have hoped the 1983 increases would slip by unnoticed.

One possible answer to this important criticism is that even though straightforward limits may favour incumbents as a whole, some special provisos that accompany limits may favour one party over others. The tensions this generates can at times lead to an increase in limits. A party may push for a higher limit if the increase is structured in a way that helps the party and hinders its opponents. When such tilting of the playing field is impossible, resorting to lower limits for all parties, without special exemptions and provisos, may be generally accepted by the club of incumbents as a tolerable compromise. Simple limits would not favour one party above another but would at least protect incumbent candidates against challengers.

For example, before ceilings were raised in 1983, in some cases, the Liberals and P.C.s came within a few percent of the limits, while the N.D.P. were generally well below the limits. Much of the N.D.P.'s campaign effort came from volunteer labour, which the law did not count as part of expenditure. The P.C.s and the Liberals may have worried that inflation would erode the real value of what they were allowed to spend, but would not touch the uncounted category of volunteer labour. Indexing the limits to inflation would at least have preserved the relative advantages of the parties. Such a compromise would not have been necessary had the value of all resources come under official audit. Then it would have served the interests of all incumbents to set an unchanging nominal limit; every year inflation would have lowered its real value and the greater harm would have come to challengers.[6]

---

6   One would then have expected the N.D.P. to oppose limit increases in the early 1980s but they did not. Perhaps they went along with the increase

Of all parties the P.C.s seem most opposed to limits, but their opposition is very particular. Norm Atkins (1990), a senior Conservative figure, has argued for higher ceilings of a special sort. He believes that campaign labour donated by the self-employed should be exempt from spending limits. His party echoes similar sentiments. Bill C-79, a major reform of the Canada Elections Act, failed to pass in 1988 because the Conservative government insisted that so-called paid-volunteer labour (of which they were the greatest users) remain exempt from limits.[7] The debates on Bill C-79 (see *House of Commons Debates*, March 16, 1988) suggest that each party has a different idea of how far limits should be raised and of what items should be exempt. A party's favourite exemptions will be for spending on campaign activities it has found profitable (volunteer labour for New Democrats, paid-volunteer labour for Conservatives).

Unfortunately, in the Canadian case, it is difficult to do more than speculate by use of examples because of an understanding between the parties that changes to campaign law can only be made by unanimous consent of the House (Jacques Gibeault, *House of Commons Debates*, 1988, p.13, 816). No proper record exists of the bargaining and discussions that go into changing the act. More concrete evidence comes from the U.S. where legislative roll calls are on open record. In an enticing study, Bender (1988) found that Congressmen were likelier to vote on amendments to the Federal Election Campaign Act restricting spending, the lower their marginal product of campaign spending was, from which he concluded spending limits would favour congressional incumbents and reduce political competition.

---

because spending limits were only one area of reform. Bill C-169 amended 37 parts of the Canada Elections Act, and the Commons passed it unanimously. Large pieces of law (so-called omnibuses) can only pass without protest if legislators bargain. Each party will insist on certain points and let others go. Unanimous consent in the Commons may hide the fact that such "logrolling" went into the omnibus. If the limit rise hurt the NDP, they may have received compensation in other parts of the act big enough to make them want to go along with it. This, however, is still an open question and the above is only one possible interpretation.

7   Under the present law, an expense on labour provided at less than its commercial value is exempt from the limit. (See S2(1) of the Canada Elections Act for a definition of election expenses.)

Another difficult question for the self-interest view of campaign finance legislation is why, if they are so good for incumbents, were limits passed only in 1974 and not at Confederation in 1867? The self-interest argument is that incumbents want limits because challengers get more votes for their money. This, however, may not have always been the case, or at least the difference in productivity may not have been so great and the money-raising abilities of incumbents may have been more formidable. Consider the case of the incumbent who gets half as many votes per dollar as the challenger, but who can raise four times as much. A limit that halves the incumbent's spending would not even bind the challenger, but would reduce the incumbent's vote. No incumbent would want limits under these circumstances. Such circumstances may have prevailed until television spread wide enough to let obscure challengers (such as John F. Kennedy) mount sudden, successful challenges.

Conclusion

Campaign spending regulation is widely viewed as a means of fostering political competition. The arguments presented here suggest a different interpretation. The picture that emerges is one of incumbents using government money to run a continuous campaign *between* elections during which they try to cement their constituents' support. This inter-election spending makes them less potent campaigners by the time of the election because it exhausts the potential of what their money can achieve—their spending runs into diminishing returns. A spending limit protects their initial advantage by reducing the more productive challenger outlays, and it reduces incumbents' costs by sparing them the need to fight expensive battles in response to the threat of strong challengers. Limits and franking privileges act as barriers to entry and may not "level the playing field" or encourage candidates to use resources imaginatively.

Significantly, it is misleading to judge the efficiency and competitiveness of an electoral system by a simple index such as the turnover rate of incumbents. Attention should instead go to asking if the rules of elections are set so that information can flow freely and voters can punish incumbents for bad performance, and policy should aim to promote these conditions. Many of this chapter's conclusions follow from the assumption that campaign advertising brings important information to voters. The next chapter looks at the role of information in greater detail.

Chapter 4

The Role of Information in Elections

Abstract

Campaign spending transmits many different kinds of information. Spending buys advertisements which may explicitly describe candidate platforms, but ads that promote an "image" can be a convenient shorthand for this type of message. The size of campaign expenditure can also transmit information to voters. A candidate may be well-endowed because many contributors with inside information approve; thus spending can be a signal of political worth. Voters use opinion polls as guides to what others think and this information helps them make decisions. The general effect of money in elections is to lower the cost of information to voters. There are many inexpensive ways for candidates to send valuable signals that allow large numbers of people to coordinate their actions. In general these signals will be beneficial because our system provides politicians with strong incentives to furnish voters with accurate, if not complete, information about themselves.

Introduction

A restriction on the amount of money a person or a group can spend on political communication during a campaign necessarily reduces the quantity of expression by restricting the number of issues discussed, the depth of their exploration and the size of the audience reached. This is because virtually every means of communicating ideas in today's mass society requires expenditure of money (*Buckley vs. Valeo*, U.S. Supreme Court, 1976).

CANDIDATES AND CONSTITUENTS LEARN ABOUT each other during election campaigns. Everyone agrees in principle that more knowledge is better, which is why spending ceilings and restrictions on how and when money is to be spent are always legislated with apologies for the freedom of speech they take away. Such apologies seldom accompany government subsidies to candidates, individual contributions limits, and bans on opinion polls because these regulations do not seem directed at the exchange of information. This simple slotting of the types of rules that interfere with knowledge ignores that election information moves through channels other than television and radio advertisements. Polls are a valuable way of finding out what other people think about the candidates and of drawing information from those thoughts. Contributions themselves are a form of opinion poll, and subsidies interfere with the quality of information contained in contributions.

Election law will overlook these possibilities if it is not guided by a sense of how people collect information and why candidates choose to transmit it. A democratic electoral system gives challenging candidates a strong incentive to provide voters with the type of information they value most. "Image advertising" and complicated policies shrunk into slogans seem to violate the traditional ideal of candidates who spell out their platforms for voters, but are, in fact, intelligent responses to the problem of communicating with people who do not have time to explore all the details. Voters also get knowledge from independent sources such as newspapers and opinion polls, and by listening to what others think, which helps them put together a picture of the candidates at little personal cost.

In this chapter I explain how campaigns send valuable signals to voters and how voters evaluate the truth and content of messages they receive. Politicians have strong incentives to provide information at low cost to voters, while voters have methods of evaluating political signals. These signals help large numbers of voters to coordinate their actions at little cost. When voters use election information to act in concert they can impose discipline on their representatives, which is why policy makers with the public's interest at heart must be alert to the effect that campaign regulation will have on the flow of information. Spending limits are obvious threats to knowledge but other laws such as restrictions on opinion polls, contributions limits, and campaign subsidies can also do damage.

The political incentives to inform the public

Voters suffer when they lose information, because without it they cannot judge which candidates are worthy of election. Candidates are needed because most issues before governments are too complicated to decide by referendum. The majority of voters are not well placed to evaluate policies because it is too hard to see where the costs and benefits are coming from. As Nelson (1976) wrote, "the minority decides on the form of its gain to make it difficult for the majority to realize that it is losing as the minority gains. It is in the interests of a maximizing minority to make it hard for the majority to get information, given the crucial constraint of majority information on minority gains. . . . The minority must take its gains where the issue can be easily obscured." For example, how many of us feel cheated by the extra three cents per carton we pay the local milk marketing board? We need candidates to research these abuses (abuses due perhaps to the incumbent dealing with special interests) and to show us why prices are suspiciously high. Information about the best candidate for the job can make an important difference to how well the public is served.

The complexity of issues is why campaigns devote so much energy to promoting candidates and talk so little about the details of platforms; most voters do not have the time or ability to be interested. When attention focuses on an issue it is usually because the choices are clear. Referendums are the purest example. Matsusaka (1991) argues that electoral systems tend to decide obvious distributional questions—such as tax reform—by referendum, that is, without the help of an intermediary such as a politician. People systematically inform themselves on these issues because the benefits or costs are large and evident. Questions of economic efficiency (should we regulate pollution?) and foreign policy are usually decided by elected representatives. The focus on candidates to the apparent neglect of issues is a rational response to the cost of learning.

It is very expensive for voters to go out and collect political information. They get it passively, by reading newspapers or through various groups to which they belong. It is especially hard for large groups to inform themselves because of what is known as the "free rider" problem—the gains to the majority as a whole of learning about the milk monopoly may be huge but it is hard to coerce every member to pay his share of the bill for finding this out.[1] The majority can overcome this problem by appointing an agent (the politician) to collect and advertise this information. In return, they promise to vote for him and to indulge him in the use of the resources of office (free plane rides, large staff, subsidized living). The politician is really someone who tells the majority, "I will inform you about the abuses of the system but in turn I must be allowed some lesser abuses of my own."

Voters are not all interested in the same topics nor are they completely ignorant at the start of a campaign, which may mean that much of what one hears and reads may be irrelevant or redundant. Election laws that interfere with communications would have a large margin of error and might not be as harmful as I am suggesting here. However, what voters see and hear will not be superfluous if politicians and the independent media channel election information to those who need and value it most, for then they will cater to voters' interests and fill gaps in their knowledge without waste. The test of this notion according to Nelson (1976) is that

> Advertising for a candidate will be distributed most heavily among those who would be likely to vote for the candidate if they knew the candidate's position.

In other words, candidates will supply their information where it is most valued. This is an indirect test, in the sense that when information has value for a group, the candidate who holds that information will get his biggest return at the polls from targeting that group. A corollary is that newspapers will tend to publish news that interests its audience.

Nelson (1976) found that in the 1968 presidential race Democrats advertised most heavily in those areas likely to support them and that

---

1   However, see Wittman (1989, p. 1407) for a counterexample.

editorial positions in support of Humphrey were most frequently found in the same areas. McAllister (1985) found that in the 1979 British general election, "11% of Conservative voters reported being influenced by a Conservative broadcast, but only 3% by a labour broadcast. In 1983, voters were again more influenced by their own party's [political broadcasts]." A prediction of Nelson's theory is that a binding spending limit would leave voters with unsatisfied desire for information. In a study of the 1988 Canadian federal race, in which limits bound many candidates, 70% of Canadians said they did not have enough information on free trade—the central issue of the campaign (Pammett, 1990).

Relevance to policy

Voters value information about candidates and events because it helps them to keep an eye on government. When a law interferes with information, certain groups in society gain at the expense of others. Consider a restriction on the number of hours a politician can advertise on television. As explained in Chapter 2, this interferes with his optimal "spending mix" (his cleverest use of a given sum of campaign money). Television is a cheap and effective way of spreading a message. It is cheap for consumers because it is a minor part of a larger activity i.e. watching a program (Nelson, 1971).[2] A limit on the number of hours politicians can advertise discriminates against the majority by interfering with this efficient channel of communication between voters and politicians. The reduced flow of information fosters a climate in which politicians and special interest groups can strike deals undisturbed by angry publicity. In such a climate the returns to lobbying are greater, and perversely, even though a limit could decrease what is spent on a campaign, may actually increase the amount of money society spends on political activity because special interests lobby more (a costly activity) due to the increased returns (see Nelson, 1976).[3]

---

2   In Great Britain, television is the main source of political information during campaigns. In 1979, 75% of voters surveyed had seen a party political broadcast, whereas only 16% had heard one on the radio, and 4% had attended a party rally (McAllister, 1985).

3   In India and Turkey, where it is probably very costly to advertise against political misdeeds, Kreuger has estimated that up to 7% of gross national

Who benefits will also depend on the definition of spending. If the law excludes the value of volunteer labour from expenditures, parties that rely heavily on volunteers will advance. This is perhaps why the N.D.P. put pressure on the minority Trudeau government of 1972-74 to strike volunteer labour from the incipient statutory limits on spending.

Content in political advertising

> The sole purpose of campaigning is to inform the electorate about the position of the candidates on various issues. In light of spiralling campaign costs it would appear that access to public office is becoming dependent upon a candidate's financial means rather than the worthiness of his/her political stance (Ontario Commission on Election Finances, 1988, p. 20).

Politicians direct information where it is most valued and package it in digestible morsels. This often provokes the complaint (implied in the above quote) that candidates do not talk about the issues and are too busy projecting an image in advertisements that convey no useful information. Much of campaign spending is a waste (a "deadweight loss")—the public does not gain and neither do candidates. Candidates are compelled to spend heavily in static battles of attrition. It is important not to be outspent because, as students of campaign advertising put it, "persuasive communications" can change attitudes. Voters respond to superficial advertising that keeps the candidate's ideas and platform in a haze, so that through advertisements candidates can increase voter demand for their services (this is similar to Galbraith's argument that firms can brainwash consumers with advertising to create demand for useless products).

A less despondent interpretation is that the high cost of transmitting and absorbing knowledge leads candidates and voters to communicate in a political shorthand which appears vacuous but which has real content. For example, the party name is a simple label and seal of quality

---

product is wasted by lobbyists in their pursuit of government protection and quotas. This pursuit is possible in part because incumbents are less exposed to the public and have greater leeway to deal with special interests. The returns to successful lobbying are therefore greater and more effort is expended in what Bhagwati (1982) has called directly unproductive profit-seeking activities.

that can do for campaign promises and policies what the Good House-keeping seal does for a new appliance. There may be also be clues in endorsements and in an "image." Consider two competing politicians who choose to market themselves as soft drinks, running their campaigns on the merit that they have all the ingredients to do a good job and that a star-studded cast of thousands is willing to sing a jingle about the candidates on television. Is the money they spend a social waste? Is the campaign manipulative? That depends on what people read into the message. Perhaps it impresses me that people of distinction in the community are willing to endorse a candidate. If I am too busy to read the newspapers, and weigh all the issues, and research the candidates, the seemingly superficial information in the commercial could be precious.

Politicians pay so much attention to their reputations—perhaps at the expense of presenting clear platforms—because endorsement is an important key to success.[4] As Wittman (1989) writes:

> A voter needs to know little about the actions of his congressman in order to make intelligent choices in the election. It is sufficient for the voter to find a person or organization(s) with similar preferences and then ask advice on how to vote. For example, people who like to hunt are more likely to read the literature from the National Rifle Association than from an organization attempting to ban guns. . . . Voters can also look at the list of campaign contributors (who typically make their endorsements public) and infer the characteristics of the candidates' policies (pro or con). That is, interest group endorsements are like signals in the market and provide strong cues about candidates' preferences."

Wittman makes the intriguing point that campaign contributions are endorsements that carry information, meaning that there is information in the amount of money spent on a campaign quite independent of

---

4   Kornberg, Mishler, and Clarke (1982) find evidence in the 1979 Canada Election Survey that voters care directly about issues as well as candidate images, but that this is more true of educated and politically active voters who presumably do not have to rely as much on candidates' images to judge the candidates. Kornberg, Mishler, and Clarke also warn that voters may rationalize having voted by convincing themselves it was the issues and not the images of the candidates that figured in their selection.

how that money is spent. An extreme example is the candidate who buys television ads in which only his name appears. What are voters to make of this? What information does the act of spending carry? Voters could infer that the candidate has the support of many private individual contributors. Each contributor can share his own insight, or his special knowledge of why the candidate is good, by giving; thus, each dollar reflects a bit of information. Hayek (1945) and later Lucas (1972) suggested that something like this happens in economic markets. The price of wheat today may reflect farmers' educated guesses about the weather next season. Casual observers can pull some part of this "signal" from the price of wheat to forecast the weather! Similarly, outside investors in the stock market may see the price of gold rising and may decide to buy gold because the change reflects the informed bids of gold mining specialists who believe the price will continue to rise. In the same sense that price may signal the quality of a stock, contributions can be a measure of the candidate.

Spending is not a sign of public endorsement when it comes from the candidate's personal wealth, but it can still carry information. By using his own fortune a candidate shows that he is confident enough of his own political talents to invest in himself. The founders of new companies often invest heavily in their own enterprises to convince outside investors to buy equity. There are returns to putting one's money where one's mouth is because there are risks (the company may fail). This is what makes personal spending a credible signal (Myers and Majluf, 1984).

Relevance to policy

If the above arguments paint an accurate picture then public subsidies to campaigns, and spending (or contributions) limits can reduce what voters know. A subsidy corrupts the signal carried in the amount a candidate spends. If voters are uncertain about the size of government subsidies they will have more trouble figuring out what campaign spending means (is it due to endorsements or due to the subsidy?). This may not be much of a problem because the formulas for calculating official subsidies are public knowledge and because voters can probably get an adequate idea of how much support the candidates have by looking at how much they spend relative to each other. A more serious threat comes from contributions and spending limits. Not only do limits make it hard for candidates to speak (their obvious shortcoming), but they stifle the kind of private knowledge about the candidates that contributors can provide.

Polls

Opinion polls are another device people use to draw information from a campaign. They can be an invaluable guide to what others think and thus to one's own actions. The rise of polls is a sign of how valuable a service they provide; in 1980 only two national media polls appeared, compared to 12 in 1984; polls were the centre of campaign coverage in 84 and were in 20% of election news reports (Fletcher, 1984, p. 170). Many complain that polls turn elections into a horse race and divert attention from the issues. But recent research suggests that a succession of polls can reveal where the candidates stand and what the issues are.

Suppose I am registered to vote in the 1988 federal election, that I favour free trade, and that I am not sure how the Conservatives stand on this issue, but I am aware a majority of voters know and that they also happen to be free trade supporters. The first poll of the campaign will show an advantage for Conservatives. I will conclude that these informed people are responsible and that the conservatives are probably free traders. I will then have a clue to which side to pick.

McKelvey and Ordeshook (1984, 1985) refined this idea to show that an uninformed voter can learn from a sequence of polls approximately where a candidate stands on the scale of an issue (e.g. should military spending be $1 billion, or $2 billion, or $3 billion, and so on?).[5] They tested this hypothesis on samples of university student volunteers. Some of the students were told beforehand what positions the imaginary candidates held. Others were left uninformed but were paid to study the polls and try to figure out the positions. They found that the number of uninformed subjects who correctly identified the positions of imaginary candidates rose to 58% after the first poll, 79% in the second, and 81% in the third and final poll.

---

5   See also McKelvey and Page, 1990.

Voters can also use polls to vote strategically. For example, Fletcher (1984) surmises that Quebecers shifted some of their allegiance from the P.C.s to the N.D.P. towards the end of the 1984 election as it became clear the P.C.s would win a crushing majority (they did so to put some limit on the P.C.'s mandate). In the same election the Liberal leader John Turner contested the traditionally Conservative riding of Vancouver–Quadra: "Knowing that the election was won, a number of previously conservative voters . . . decided it would be good for the riding or the country to have a party leader representing Vancouver–Quadra. The knowledge derived from the published polls made such strategic voting possible" (Fletcher, 1984, p. 172).

Relevance to policy

The influence of polls is now widely recognized and regulators are starting to look for ways in which to control this rich source of information. Bill C-79, which failed to pass in parliament in 1988, would have amended the Canada Elections Act to oblige any published poll result to identify who commissioned and paid for the poll. This putative measure was mild compared to some proposed in testimony to the 1990 Lortie Commission by party representatives, and by academics. Fearing that last minute, biased polls could skew outcomes unfairly, some suggested that officially appointed groups of experts should judge the integrity and competence of polls before their publication (see the panel discussion by the Canadian Study of Parliament Group, 1990, pp. 14-17).

The media were among the few to oppose regulation, on grounds that polls were a form of free speech that none had the competence to regulate. As I have argued here, the value of free speech is that it carries information. Complying with edicts to submit to tests of competence would increase the cost of polling and thereby reduce the amount done. As a result, voters would have less information to go by.

Polls may be biased, as many fear, but it is not clear that concentrating the power to stop their publication in the hands of a government panel would improve matters. Who is to judge how biased the panel is? Nor is it clear that a biased source of information will bias what the electorate believes. The next section looks at this point in detail.

Truth in political advertising

My insistence that campaigns convey useful information in convenient format may seem incredibly naive to hard-bitten election observers who carry the conviction that politicians are rascals ready to tell the public anything. Some scepticism is inevitable for a century in which Nazis and Communists have raised the political lie to an art. Its seedbed, however, has been in countries without competitive elections, where the incentives to be truthful are seldom strong. Western democracies generally promote honesty by allowing consumer-voters to "repurchase" the candidate at each election. Candidates are so-called experience goods. After several purchases voters can see if they are getting what was advertised on the label and can decide to change their allegiance if unsatisfied. To paraphrase Ford, Smith, and Swasy (1990), the behaviour of politicians is influenced by the behaviour of voters, and the ultimate reason why political advertising provides information stems from the voter's knowledge of when to be sceptical of advertising claims.

Ford, Smith, and Swasy (1990) find that consumers of commercial products are sceptical of claims which they can only verify after buying the product. If the analogy carries over to voters it might explain why having a good track record is deemed important for starting and continuing a parliamentary career (see Nelson, 1976). A track record is sign that previous consumer-voters have sampled the political product to their satisfaction. Many novice candidates for Parliament present themselves only after extended tours of duty in political outposts such as city councils, school boards, and Kiwanis clubs. The reputations they establish there soothe the anxious voter poised to commit himself to a full term under a single representative.

Once in office, a lie can erode the work of years, whereas being honest and keeping promises will generate further political capital. The ferreting presence of competitors and press, eager to find unbecoming and sensational facts, may keep all but the most crooked candidates in line. In addition, dishonest candidates may not thrive because parties have a very strong incentive to choose representatives who will not embarrass them. A scandal such as Watergate can harm a party long after the culprits have retired to writing their memoirs.

Even if politicians do lie, voters may be well equipped to see through the falsehood or to deal with biased reports. Soviet citizens expertly divine truth from official balderdash, and Westerners are capable of similar insights, as Wittman (1989) describes:

> I have never met anyone who believes that the Defense Department does not exaggerate the need for defense procurement. But if everyone knows that the Defense Department will exaggerate the importance of its contributions to human welfare, then, on average, voters will sufficiently discount the Defense Department claims. Hence biased sources of information need not lead to biases in belief.

None of this proves that election campaigns will be forums of sincere and honest discussion. Voters may have rules for weighing political claims just as consumers have for goods, but even in the market for commercial products, where data are more abundant and which has been a topic of intense research for half a century, the nature and scope of these rules is not well understood (Ford, Smith, and Swasy, 1990); thus it is not clear how constrained politicians are in bending the truth. But there are indications that voters are not lambs in need of constant government guidance; some weight should be given to Wittman's point that biased sources of information need not lead to biases in belief.

Conclusion

The purpose of this chapter was to show that there are many subtle ways in which voters and candidates can communicate. Voters do not have the time to learn about issues in detail and so rely on candidate "images" and on the opinions of other voters (as reflected perhaps through polls) to evaluate the candidates. In general voters can trust election information because democratic elections give candidates incentives to be truthful, but voters are also equipped to deal with dubious claims.

Information allows voters to punish incumbents for misdeeds and to hold victorious challengers to their promises, which is why information is valued. There is, however, an important problem with this view: No one individual can possibly hope to make a difference to the electoral outcome. Of what use can information then be? The next chapter on voter participation is devoted in part to answering this criticism.

Chapter 5

Should Voter Turnout be Stimulated?

Abstract

Spending limits both increase the costs of making an intelligent choice between candidates, and affect voter turnout. Participation has no intrinsic value, but it can be a sign that voters are making efficient use of the electoral system, and that they attach worth to their vote. Government schemes such as fines or rewards may also raise turnout, but may not have the same benefits as campaign spending. Canadian and American data seem to show that campaign spending and turnout go hand in hand. I use evidence from Canadian elections to simulate the effect of a spending limit on voter turnout.

Introduction

CANADIANS DO NOT TURN OUT to vote in as great a numbers as the citizens of most other developed democracies. Table 5.1 shows that in elections held in the years around 1981, Canadian voter turnout ranked near the bottom of a list of twenty countries. Table 5.2 shows details for Canada since 1968. According to the *Montreal Gazette*, this and similar performances show that "Canada fails the test of democracy with low voter turnout" (Oct. 17, 1988). The test of democracy, however, is not as simple and severe as this. People vote or abstain for many reasons, and these reasons must be examined before abstention is condemned and participation is praised.

Table 5.1

Voter Turnout and Institutional Characteristics of 20 Democracies in the Most Recent Elections of 1981[a]

Country	Rank	Average Turnout as % of Eligible	Compulsory Voting	Eligible Required to Register
Italy	1	94%	yes	automatic
Austria	2	88	no	automatic
Belgium	2	88	yes	automatic
Sweden	2	88	no	automatic
Australia	3	86	yes	yes
Denmark	4	85	no	automatic
W. Germany	4	85	no	automatic
N. Zealand	5	83	no	yes
Finland	6	82	no	automatic
Netherlands	6	82	no	automatic
Norway	6	82	no	automatic
Israel	7	80	no	automatic
France	8	78	no	no
Spain	8	78	no	automatic
Ireland	9	77	no	automatic
U.K.	10	75	no	automatic
Japan	11	72	no	automatic
Canada	12	68	no	automatic
U.S.	13	54	no	no
Switzerland	14	44	no	automatic

[a]Adapted from Powell Jr. (1986).

Table 5.2

Probability of Casting a Decisive Vote in a
Two-Candidate Election as a Function of District Size
and the Probability *"P"* that any Given Person Votes for
Candidate 1

Probability	District Size		
P	1001	100,001	1,000,001
0.4	0.3×10^{-10}	—[a]	—[a]
0.45	0.2×10^{-3}	—[a]	—[a]
0.475	0.007	—[a]	—[a]
0.49	0.021	0.5×10^{-11}	—[a]
0.4999	0.025	0.0025	0.0008
0.5	0.025	0.0025	0.0008

[a] denotes a number less than 10^{-35}.

Note: There are two candidates in this race. Clearly the number of voters matters to whether or not one will cast the decisive ballot, but what is also important is the probability that any given voter votes for any given candidate—say Candidate 1. If there is a very even split of opinion, then *P* is close to .5 and one's chances of being the kingmaker improve.

Source: Adapted from Chamberlain and Rothschild, 1981.

The last chapter explained that voters value campaign spending because the advertisement that it buys lowers the cost of making an intelligent choice. The present chapter applies this argument to several questions: How does spending work to influence turnout? Is participation due to spending better than participation due to government schemes such as fines or subsidies? In other words, are certain types of turnout better than others? I argue that changes in turnout are a good sign if better information is the cause, but that turnout in and of itself has no significance or value for policy. Better information can stimulate participation, but it can also depress it, which makes it difficult to measure how attentive voters are by looking at a simple index such as the number of votes cast. What matters for voter welfare is the setting in which they participate (e.g. do the rules of the campaign promote a free flow of information?). The effect these rules may have on participation is mainly of academic interest.

The logic behind this surprising claim is the following: there are many competing theories and practical studies of why people vote, but most agree that differences between the candidates are a factor. People may vote because they enjoy the act of voting, but they may also decide to vote according to how different the candidates are. Why vote if both sides are the same? At the start of a campaign everyone has a prior—and perhaps very different—notion of where the candidates stand. In promoting themselves, candidates change peoples' prior beliefs. This change may lower turnout if it reveals the candidates to be more alike than was generally thought. Under different circumstances, it is also possible that more people would turn out to vote. The value of turnout is unclear because both greater and lesser turnout can be the consequence of a better-informed electorate.

Why people vote

People vote for a number of reasons, but despite 50 years of research, the prime determinants of voting are still not well understood (see Matsusaka and Palda, 1990). One could, of course, simply ask people about their voting habits. The 1965 *Canada Election Survey* did ask people for their views. The results suggested that people who thought they could influence election outcomes were likelier to participate in politics (VanLoon and Whittington, 1976, pp. 116-117). However, this sort of result is not reliable because subjects may not remember exactly what moved them at the time, or may invent explanations to justify what may seem to them a pointless act. In addition, abstainers may, out of shame, claim they voted. Instead of asking people, it may be more revealing to start with the premise that people vote because they get pleasure from the act (so-called consumption voting) and because voting is an instrument for attaining certain objectives (so-called instrumental voting). Both motives are probably grounded in the type of person the voter is. Some (Wolfinger and Rosenstone, 1980) have tried to identify the objective attributes (sex, age, education, race, etc., as opposed to opinions about one's characteristics, such as an explanation of why one did something) that make voting likely. Knowing who votes, however, is not the same as knowing why they vote. To this end some theory of what motivates people is necessary.

The Downsian Hypothesis

One popular theory, which neatly combines both instrumental and consumption reasons for voting, is due to Downs (1957). The theory has been extensively modified, and is no longer taken as literally as Downs may have intended, but its basic structure remains a good guide to the possible forces that bring voters out. It states that a person is likelier to vote the bigger the probable benefits from doing so. These benefits rise with the belief in the probability that one's vote can determine the outcome, with how different the candidates appear, in the pleasure of voting, and in the costs of voting. The following equation sums up the benefits:

Benefit = Prob x Difference + Joy – Cost

where

Benefit is the net value expected from voting. It is not the benefit of having voted, which is revealed only after the results of the election are known. The difference between the two is similar to the difference between the pleasure one anticipates from a meal and the pleasure one actually gets from eating it. The distinction is important, because we act on the gains we anticipate. The insight of Downs' approach is to seek an explanation for voting in the variables from which people build their anticipations.

Prob is the probability that any one voter can decide the outcome. It is the chance of a tie vote (which only takes one ballot to break). The greater this probability is, the greater the anticipated benefit of voting. In other words, if you think you matter to the outcome you will vote. If you do not (Prob = 0) there is no point. Empirical work takes this to mean that people vote more in races which are "close," where closeness is measured as a forecast of a candidate's margin of victory or loss.

Difference is the absolute difference between the positions of the candidates. If the important election issue is aid to Eastern

Europe, and one candidate wishes to send $1 billion, whereas the other thinks $1 million is good enough, there is a $999 million difference of opinion. If there is no difference, then the candidates are identical and there is no point in turning out; one is just as well off with either at the helm. The probability of being decisive and the difference between candidates reinforce each other. If the difference is large, a small chance of being decisive can still encourage turnout: one may not change things but the stakes are so high that one has to try. Those who vote for instrumental reasons are sensitive to closeness and difference.

Joy is the psychic pleasure that comes from voting. This is the consumption aspect of voting.

Cost is the cost of voting: the cab fare to the polling station, the money forgone from having to take the afternoon off, the annoyance of standing in line and dealing with polling officers, the annoyance of travelling through bad weather, but above all the cost of informing yourself about the candidates. This cost is lower the more candidates spend and the more involved newspeople become. The lower the cost, the bigger the net benefits of turning out are.

In Downs' model, campaign spending may increase or decrease overall district turnout, but for any given level of information **Difference** should have a positive effect. Information has an ambiguous effect for the following reason: at the start of a race potential voters have prior notions of where the candidates stand and how close the race is likely to be. Partisan advertising can upset these notions if it conveys new (though not necessarily true) information. If a voter learns that the candidates are less different than he thought, his chances of voting fall. If this individual represents the average of his district then overall turnout will also fall. But spending can work both ways; if on average people initially believe candidates to be more alike than is revealed by spending during the campaign, then turnout will rise. Downs favoured the second possibility because he thought that lack of information makes it difficult to tell the sides apart, so that initially people see few differences. In this case, new information can only increase turnout.

Almost no headway has been made in testing whether greater difference in candidate platforms stimulates turnout because there is no clear way to measure these differences. Survey evidence (Kornberg, Mishler, and Clarke, 1982) from the 1979 *Canadian Election Study* suggests that in provincial elections, on average, 33% of those eligible voted because of the issues. This is some indication that candidate positions stimulate turnout, but as the authors warned, voters may invent reasons after the fact to justify their behaviour.

As a result of these difficulties, tests of the theory have focused on the more easily measured cost and closeness components. In a test of the cost component, Matsusaka (1990) found that Californians were less likely to vote on any given issue in a referendum when more issues appeared on the ballot (presumably because it costs more to learn about many issues well enough to bother voting on them). Tests of the decisiveness component have not given consistent results (see Foster, 1984), and recent detailed survey evidence from the Canadian general elections of 1979 and 1980 show absolutely no influence of closeness on the chance that an individual votes.[1] Matsusaka and Palda (1990) built "objective" measures of closeness from actual and predicted district vote tallies (as a way of avoiding the biases that had plagued earlier studies) and matched them to individuals in the survey who came from those same districts. They then performed logistic regressions of the individual's decision to vote or abstain on the closeness measure, on objective attributes of the individual such as age, sex, education, on the intensity of the district campaign, and on communal variables such as the district's level of education, religiosity, and so on. None of the six different closeness measures they used showed any sign of influencing the decision to vote.

Even though they found no closeness effect, their study did not disprove that people vote because they think they can make a difference. It is very hard to test this prediction of the theory, because even in

---

1 Also see Barry, 1978, who studied survey data of congressional voters and found little evidence that predicted closeness influenced the individual's decision to vote.

Table 5.3

Voter Participation in Canadian Federal Elections
Since 1968

Year	Votes Cast in 1000s	Registered Voters in 1000s	Votes as a Percentage of those Registered
1968	8,218	10,861	75.7%
1972	9,975	13,001	76.7
1974	9,671	13,620	71.0
1979	11,541	15,235	75.8
1980	11,026	15,890	69.3
1984	12,638	16,775	75.3
1988	13,282	17,639	75.3

Sources: *Report of the Chief Electoral Officer for the 34th General Election (Appendices). Report of the Chief Electoral Officer for the 31st General Election*, parts I, III, and IV.

electorates of modest size the chance that any one voter is decisive rapidly approaches zero. Table 5.3 shows that in a two-candidate race with 1001 voters who each have a 0.5 chance of voting for either candidate the odds any one can be the kingmaker are 1 in 40. In a district of 100,001 the odds are 1 in 400. When the chance that anyone votes for Candidate 1 is lower or higher than 0.5 the odds of being kingmaker plummet rapidly to zero.[2] A different way of making this point is by noting that no Canadian elections have been decided by a single vote. It may still be true that people are likelier to vote if they think they can

---

2   The probability of being kingmaker depends not only on district size but also on one's assessment that any other given voter will vote for Candidate 1 or 2. If the chance of anyone voting for 1 is remote then the vote will slide to Candidate 2 and no one voter will count. But in a tight race the chance of being decisive rises.

make a difference. The problem is that there are few elections in which anyone can be decisive.[3]

The "Voting as a Moral Exercise" hypothesis

The instrumental motive in Downs' hypothesis has attracted attention because it links voting to measurable quantities—such as closeness, and spending—which election regulation can influence. But the absence of a closeness effect casts doubt on the importance of this motive.

Not wishing to abandon the attractive idea of participation for instrumental reasons, researchers have subtly redefined the benefits of voting. Coleman (1990, pp. 289-292) argues that voters participate to obey societal norms because obeying and even enforcing these norms is considered a productive activity. Norms are rules to which members of a community willingly submit in order to govern acts with wide consequences. Politeness, dress, cleanliness, are all norms that keep unpleasant natural tendencies in check. Individuals who associate regularly with each other will have some interest in enforcing these norms by punishing transgressors—perhaps with cross looks, unfriendliness, and gossip. The natural tendency not to participate in elections may also be the target of norms by a group that needs high turnout to achieve its political goals. Members of a group do not value turnout by other members for its own sake but because it helps their cause. If they can push each other to vote (not explicitly telling each other whom to vote for because it is assumed all members have similar goals) they will all gain. Each member, however, has an interest to shirk and allow others to make the effort, which is why norms are needed. By promoting the belief that voting is a moral, patriotic, democratic, duty, and that good

---

3   A more technical problem is that the data do not display much variation in decisiveness even though margins vary a lot. Consider that if Mulroney is expected to win by 10,000 votes in his constituency, an extra thousand more or less will not make much difference to your chance of being the kingmaker. So in empirical work, relating large changes in margin to turnout is really like relating minuscule changes in the chance of a making a difference, to turnout. It is not surprising then that researchers fail to find a consistent effect.

people participate, shirkers are put to shame. People who live long in a community and have many ties to friends and social organizations should be likelier to vote than wanderers, because they are easier to punish.

Unfortunately, this approach to voting has the same shortcoming as the closeness explanation; no one member of the group can hope to make a difference to the outcome by enforcing norms. There has to be a narrower, more obvious self-interest at work, and curiously morals—which are even more fundamental than norms—may be the answer. According to Frank (1988) there are important returns to being judged honest. Observing norms and behaving morally, even when no one is looking, makes people bad liars. They betray their motives in ways that are difficult to falsify (blushing is an example) and this works in their favour. However, morals are not wholly given and intrinsic. Moral fibre needs exercise to keep in tone. Futile acts of unsung propriety such as not littering, or recycling waste paper, are good exercises. We do not refrain from throwing gum foil on the street because we fear it will spoil the neighbourhood (it does not—unless one performs the act in Switzerland), but because it is littering. Behaviour and morals each work on the other which is why, as Etzioni (188, p.71) writes,

> one or more illicit acts are followed by bouts of morally approved behaviour, and/or an increased search for commitment to "rehabilitation" (or atonement) via morally approved behaviour.

Another futile act, as the probabilities of Table 5.3 show, is voting. Without morals in mind, it is difficult in many cases to understand why anyone should vote, let alone inform themselves about the candidates. To the moral voter it is important to vote for the best candidate; simply voting at random will not do. To know who the best is, information is needed. Without it, candidates are hard to tell apart and the incentive to vote disappears because there is no longer a morally correct choice that needs to be made. The pursuit of such abstract goals leads to solid results. Even if no one believes that one ballot can change events, the platforms and reputations of candidates affect the outcome and turnout, as does any information—conveyed perhaps by campaign spending—that sharpens these differences. Viewing voting as a moral exercise avoids part of the trouble which Downs (1957) had in explaining why people should care about information in elections in which they cannot make a difference, and provides a rational explanation for what appears to be a pointless act.

The evidence

There are other approaches to the study of voting behaviour which do not dwell on morals, information, and norms, but they are not reviewed here.[4] Instead, I have restricted myself to understanding how campaign spending and other forces which affect information might work. In principle, more information can work both ways. To make stronger claims, further assumptions about the content of party advertising and the way people form their prior beliefs are needed. For example, suppose that "most of every party's emanations are either attacks on its opponents or defenses of itself, so it emphasizes the very elements from which party differentials are formed" (Downs, 1957, pp. 226-227), and that people initially believe the candidates to be similar (perhaps for want of information). In this case, campaign spending would convey that the candidates are less alike than most thought and would *increase* turnout.

Data from several countries do in fact show that high turnout and spending go together (Denver and Hands, 1974) but this in itself does not mean that spending stimulates turnout. It may be that contributions are high in districts with many wealthy constituents and that the rich are likelier to vote than the poor, in which case the personal wealth of constituents is the reason for the big expenditures and for the high turnout. One underlying cause (personal wealth) makes two remote variables (spending and turnout) appear directly linked, or "spuriously correlated." To find the true relation between spending and turnout, the effect of other forces in the system must be accounted for. Studies that take note of the many possible reasons for voting are able to measure its "partial influence," that is, its effect when all other factors are constant. Perhaps the first such study was by Denver and Hands (1974) who found that spending stimulated turnout in British general elections. For the U.S., Patterson and Caldeira (1983) found that spending has a

---

4   See Caldeira, Patterson, and Markko (1985) for a survey.

significant effect on turnout in state elections. Caldeira, Patterson and Markko (1985) found the same for congressional races, as did Capron and Kruseman (1988) for presidential races. Chapman and Palda (1984) estimated that a one cent increase in spending per registered voter in the 1973 Quebec provincial elections led to an additional 14.7 votes per riding being cast on average. The electoral districts had on average 34,219 registered voters, thus, a one cent increase per capita would represent an increase in campaign spending by all major party candidates of $324.19. The cost of each one of these extra votes is then $324.19/14.7, or $23.23.

Using a survey of 1,102 Canadians interviewed after the 1979 Canadian general election which they merged with district level data, Matsusaka and Palda (1990) found that a one dollar rise in campaign spending per capita led to a 12% increase in the probability that any given eligible constituent would vote. This means that an extra dollar per head will bring out 0.12x54,025, or 6,483 extra voters (54,025 is the average number of registered voters), and that the cost of each extra vote is $12.[5]

They also found that educated people were likelier to turn out. Downs (1957, p. 235) argued that education lowers the costs of learning about the candidates, thereby increasing the chance of voting. Education probably lowers the costs by making it easier to draw meaning from campaign commercials and from newspaper editorials.[6]

---

5   They also found that men were 3% likelier to vote than women, that churchgoers were about 1% likelier to vote than non-churchgoers, and that those for whom French was the mother tongue were 6% less likely to vote than the average voter. Age had a significant but diminishing effect on participation; the effect of age peaked in a person's mid to late fifties and then dropped.

6   Matsusaka and Palda (1990) also found that after accounting for all these forces, there was a lot of randomness in behaviour. Their variables only captured one tenth of the forces that drive the individual to vote. The remaining nine tenths remained unexplained due either to inherent randomness in decisions or due to variables for which they had not accounted.

Government schemes to increase turnout

The model and the evidence suggest that diverse forces shape turnout; in principle information can have an ambiguous influence but in practice the data show that campaign spending and partisan activities bring people to the polls; in principle and in practice *at any given level* of information, differences between the candidates seem to have a positive effect. These possibilities make turnout a poor indicator of political health. For example, even if the electorate is perfectly informed (the democratic ideal) it may not vote at all if the candidates happen to have identical platforms. The perennially small participation rates of Canadians and Americans (compare Tables 5.1 and 5.2) may simply show that most candidates are alike, in which case there is little to choose from and little motive to participate. The press generally ignore this interpretation in favour of the easy view that voters are ill informed, apathetic, and "fail the test of democracy."

Government schemes tailored to boost participation may achieve little of worth if they are based on the narrow premise that turnout has intrinsic value. Few would argue that enforced participation in Chinese elections are a sign of anything but official terror. The bizarre Italian practice of sometimes posting the names of non-voters outside the town hall and of stamping "DID NOT VOTE FOR FIVE YEARS" on identification papers (Seton-Watson, 1983), or the Australian, Belgian, and Venezuelan systems of fining abstainers probably do little more than encourage public cynicism.[7] They may also draw uninformed voters into the picture and lead to bad political choices. It is not clear how large these effects can be but some rough idea comes from noting that turnout is roughly 10% higher in countries which punish abstention (Powell, 1980).

Government programs that lower the cost of participating and make it easier for informed voters to use their knowledge are preferable to programs that raise the costs of abstaining. Fines attract uninformed constituents eager to vote simply to avoid punishment. Schemes that lower costs are likelier to entice informed constituents poised on the

---

7   Italy ranks low in political satisfaction and voters have unfavourable attitudes to the electoral system (U.S. General Accounting Office 1990).

brink of indifference between voting and abstaining. Mail-ballot elections are among the more daring schemes that try to make voting easier. They have been used in some American school district elections where

Table 5.4

Simulated Levels of Voter Turnout for
Various Hypothetical Levels of Total District
Spending

Hypothetical Spending by all Candidates ($)	Hypothetical Spending per Eligible Voter ($)	Simulated Turnout
$54,843[a]	$1.02[b]	40,926[c]
50,000	0.93	40,342[d]
40,000	0.74	39,110
30,000	0.56	37,943
20,000	0.37	36,711
10,000	0.19	35,479
5,000	0.09	34,311

[a]$54,843 was the sum of spending by all candidates in the average federal electoral district (f.e.d.) in 1979. Numbers below it are hypothetical aggregate spending limits.

[b]$1.02 is the actual sum of spending by all candidates per registered voter in the average f.e.d. in 1979. The average number of registered voters per f.e.d. in 1979 was 54,025. Numbers below it are hypothetical spending divided by 54,025.

[c]40,926 was the turnout in the average f.e.d in 1979. Numbers below it are simulated turnouts had aggregate spending (given in the leftmost column) been lower.

[d]This and all numbers below it are calculated as follows:
Simulated turnout=40,926 – 0.12 x (fall in spending per voter) x (registered voters) where 0.12 is the % change in district turnout for every dollar change in district spending per registered voter.

Source: This table is based on the findings of Matsusaka and Palda, 1990.

it is found that participation is between 20% and 40% higher and that the administrative costs to the organizers is at least 32% lower than under conventional balloting (U.S. General Accounting Office, 1990, pp. 37-38). However, government programs to inform voters of their rights and of the election date are of less certain value. The United States General Accounting Office (1990, pp. 43-48) found little evidence that voter information activities such as announcing registration drives and registration deadlines increased turnout. If these results apply to Canada, then perhaps more detailed reasons should be found for our expensive attempts to educate the electorate (The Chief Electoral Officer spent $4.5 million during the 1988 federal election on the Voter Information Program—making his Office the fourth biggest election spender after the N.D.P.) than the Chief Electoral Officer's "conviction that the electorate has a right to be informed about their constitutional right to vote and of the opportunities which they have to exercise that right" (Hamel, 1989, p. 29).

Instead of promoting turnout as an object of national pride election law should keep from interfering with the flow of information between candidates and constituents. As argued in the previous chapters, spending ceilings are a particularly bad form of interference. The statistics in the present chapter suggest that a complete ban on spending in Canadian elections could diminish turnout at the constituency level by 6,000 votes on average (see Table 5.4). In such a case the lowered turnout would be a sign that voters have been denied some information and would be cause for alarm.

Conclusion

Voter turnout is a symptom with many possible causes. Whether the symptom indicates health or disease hinges on a deeper diagnosis. Evidence from Canada and the U.S. suggests that spending limits would lower voter turnout. The low turnout does no harm in itself, unless one believes in the intrinsic value of the voting act. Harm comes from cutting the supply of information about candidates to voters. A spending limit does this by increasing the costs to voters of informing themselves about the differences between candidates. Getting people back to the polls with subsidies or fines is pointless because in the process nobody learns anything new about the campaign. A more productive course is to lower the cost of voting to informed voters through a scheme such as mail balloting.

Chapter 6

Limits on Advocacy Group Advertising[1]

Abstract

Incumbent campaign spending is less potent than challenger spending. Advocacy groups often spend on behalf of challengers. To protect themselves, incumbents impose spending limits and give political parties the sole right to advertise. Advocacy groups lower the costs to voters of getting messages across to politicians. However, they may also distort the information the electorate gets because they may not share the same incentives mainstream parties have to appear balanced and reasonable. Their regulation has a long history in Canada and is one of the main issues in the election reform debate.

Introduction

IN 1989 THE EAST BLOC rid itself of communist dictatorship. The elections that followed in Czechoslovakia, Hungary, Poland, and Bulgaria were remarkable free-for-alls. In each country, major parties that the

---

1   In Canada "single issue group" and "third-party" are also used to refer to private citizens or groups who join a campaign on behalf of a candidate or an issue.

communists had banished returned in triumph and dozens of small single-issue parties and groups sprang up to champion the rights of ecology, beer-lovers, gypsies, and the erotic lifestyle.[2] Activists from every centre and fringe assailed each other with loudspeakers, posters, pamphlets, and newspaper adverts, and won the admiration of Western observers for snapping democracy back to its senses with bracing whiffs of criticism and debate.

Canadians watched in approval, even as some manoeuvred to muzzle free speech on their own terrain. The Royal Commission on Electoral Reform and Party Financing toured the country in 1990 and heard what academics, private citizens, and organizations thought should be done about so called advocacy groups. The overwhelming opinion was well summarized by the Council of Canadians: "Unrestricted third party participation in elections is a clear and present danger for Canadian societal values. The electoral process can, is and will be abused if no immediate steps are taken" (*Lortie Commission Hearings*, March 12, 1990, p. 7).

The tendency Canadians have to regulate anything noisy or brash finds unpleasant and dangerous expression in the move to restrict advertising to political parties during election campaigns. This chapter explains how the controversy came to its present pass, and suggests that the common arguments against advocacy groups are a thin but popular veneer, which legislators and influence-seekers use to cover self-serving motives. Incumbents need to mute advocacy groups to ensure that spending limits on candidates remain useful barriers to competition. Advocacy groups (which are similar to policy groups in that their members, often acting out of a moral conviction, seek to influence policy in a general way rather than expecting a direct return for their efforts) are a danger to incumbents because they can spend on behalf of the restricted challenger. They are also a danger to special-interest lobbies (who do expect that their efforts will generate a specific, direct return of some kind for their members) who do not like to be exposed, and to advocacy groups who side with incumbents.

---

2   I am referring here to Czechoslovakia's "Green", "Friends of Beer," "Romany," and "Independent Erotic" parties.

The law on advocacy group spending

Two sections of Canada's election law make breathtaking reading:

> 72. (1) Every printed advertisement, handbill, placard, poster or dodger that promotes or opposes the election of a registered political party or candidate and that is displayed or distributed during an election by or on behalf of a registered party or a candidate shall indicate that it was authorized by the registered agent of the party...
>
> 70. (1) Everyone other than
>
>> (a) a candidate, official agent or any other person acting on behalf of a candidate's actual knowledge and consent, or
>>
>> (b) a registered agent of a registered party acting within the scope of his authority as such or other person acting on behalf of a registered party with the actual knowledge and consent of an officer thereof
>
> who between the date of issue of the writ for an election and the day immediately following polling day, incur election expenses is guilty of an offence against this Act.

In other words, no individual or group may spend money to express an opinion if candidates do not wish it.

These extraordinary rules sprang from the 1966 Barbeau Committee's recommendation that only registered parties and candidates be allowed to buy airtime to advertise for one side or against the other. One member of the committee stated that otherwise the effort to control election expenses would be meaningless (Medhurst, 1984, p. 445). The Chappel Committee of 1971 said the same and in 1974 the Canada Elections Act was amended by the Election Expenses Act (Bill C-203) to include Section 70.1 (quoted above). This section forgave anyone who claimed to advertise in good faith (*bona fides*) for a cause or an issue, and not to directly promote or oppose the officially registered contestants.

In 1978, the Crown brought suit against a trade union official who hired a plane to tow a banner inscribed "Vote as You Will, but not Liberal OHC Local 767 CUPE," over the riding of Ottawa-Carleton during the October 1976 by-election (*Regina vs. Roach*, 1978). The union official claimed the defence of *bona fides* provided by s.70.1(4) and the judge dismissed the case on grounds that "the fundamental principle of our parliamentary democracy [is] that there be freedom of public discussion of public affairs" (quoted from Paltiel, 1979, p. 24). The crown failed to overturn the decision by appeal to a higher court.

Jean-Marc Hamel, the Chief Electoral officer, argued in his 1983 report that the *bona fide* defence shot a hole through election expense barriers. The danger was that a group could promote a candidate while claiming that it was doing nothing more than promoting a cause. He urged Parliament either to abolish the defence or to qualify it to prevent abuse in words that nonetheless protected free speech. After Hamel's report was unanimously endorsed by an ad-hoc parliamentary committee of paid (mostly non-elected) party professionals, Parliament abolished the defence by passing Bill C-169.[3] Sections 70.1 and 72 as quoted above, became the final word on advocacy group advertising.

The bill is a curious piece of work. It was passed without question or debate, within a week of its first reading in the House of Commons by the same government and opposition who only a year earlier had repatriated the constitution from the U.K. and had written the Canadian Charter of Rights.[4] Section 2(b) of the Charter proclaimed that everyone has the "freedom of thought, belief, opinion and expression, including freedom of the press and other media communication." If Parliament had forgotten its own words and their meaning, the Alberta Supreme Court would soon remind them.

The Medhurst ruling

Early in 1984, the National Citizens' Coalition brought a suit against the Crown in the Supreme Court of Alberta. They submitted that the amendments favoured the established parties to the detriment of new parties and independent candidates, and that they harmed public participation in elections by regulating the campaign expenses of advocacy

---

3   Bill C-169 contained 37 proposals to amend the Act, among which were the raising of spending limits, more generous campaign subsidies, and changes in political broadcasting rules. The advocacy group proposal was one of many sweeping changes in the Bill.

4   See Paltiel (1988) for a good account of how quickly the Bill made it through the House of Commons.

groups (Hiebert, 1989). Their formal charge was that the amendments violated the freedom of speech and the right to an informed vote guaranteed in Sections 2(b) and 3 of the Charter of Rights. But two things tilted the scales against them. First, in 1982, Justice Bernier of the Quebec Provincial Court had ruled that the Centrale de L'enseignement du Quebec had violated the province's ban on advocacy group advertising during elections. The Court ruled that "freedom of expression is not equivalent to freedom of expenditure" and that the election law limits "not the right of free speech but the right to spend money to express oneself" (Paltiel, 1989, p. 61). Second, the Crown was prepared to use its resources to call many expert witnesses from both Canada and the U.S. to testify.

The Crown's defence was that the amendments were the result of many years of legislative effort to make the procedures governing the election of Members of Parliament fair and equal (Medhurst, 1984, p. 441). The earlier version of the Canada Elections Act was not fair to candidates because it forced them to obey a spending limit which advocacy groups could ignore. An expert witness maintained that the electorate held parties accountable for their acts but that special interests escaped this stricture (Medhurst, 1984, p. 448).[5] The Crown did not see the law as a limit on freedom of expression. In fact, the law promoted a greater exchange of opinions and ideas by banning the biased publicity of well-endowed special interests.

The Crown's theme was that of the reigning Trudeau government. Advocacy groups were irresponsible wildcat operators who came shooting from the hip, mesmerizing voters and leaving a grisly trail of political casualties. Parties—the sole legitimate representatives of the people—needed special laws to protect them from unbalanced attacks. Canadian politics were, after all, grounded in the "principle of equality," which held that any political advantage won by spending money was bad.[6] Spending should be the strict privilege of registered parties and it

---

5   This was the report of Professor John Courtney, exhibit #127.

6   Trudeau said that the restriction on advocacy groups "which originated with this government in the early 70s, was written for a specific purpose, which was to destroy the inequality which arose from the power of money. . . . It is an amendment to ensure that the Citizens' Coalition, or any other

should be strictly limited. In ceding this doubtful aspect of free speech—which few had the resources to take advantage of in any case—citizens would participate in more informative elections which would actually cost less.

Justice Medhurst did not concur. His opinion was that the amendments limited freedom of expression. He was not satisfied with the Crown's claim that mischief or harm would come of advocacy group advertising and he warned that "Fears or concerns of mischief that may occur are not adequate reasons for imposing limitations." He added that "the true test of free expression to a society is whether it can tolerate criticism of its fundamental values and institutions" (Medhurst, 1984, p. 453). Medhurst passed this judgement on June 25, 1984, only a few days before John Turner became leader of the reigning Liberal Party and two weeks before he called a general election. The Liberal government did not appeal the ruling because it had to concentrate its attention on the campaign. Even though the judgement voided the disputed sections of the Act only in Alberta, the Attorney General of Canada decided that he would not enforce a federal law that did not bind all citizens.[7] But the Liberal justice minister, Donald Johnston, warned that if advocacy groups abused their new privilege, a returning Liberal government would surely revive the legislation in another form (Hiebert, 1989).

The hidden agenda behind Bill C-169

The Alberta case is not unique. In 1976 the U.S. Supreme Court heard the case of *Buckley vs. Valeo* which was a class action suit challenging provisions of the 1974 Federal Election Campaign Act that limited freedom of expression in the electoral marketplace. The Court ruled that spending limits on candidates and advocacy groups violated the First Amendment's guarantee of free speech. An expert witness for the

---

group with a lot of money, do not controvert the spirit of the law" (Hiebert, 1989).

7   It was also the opinion of lawyers for the National Citizens Coalition, that the advocacy group provisions of Bill C-169 would not stand up to constitutional challenges in other provinces (related by the president of the coalition).

Crown in the National Citizens' trial was quick to dismiss the relevance of the American example, citing America's exceptional devotion to pure free speech (Medhurst, 1984, p. 451) as one that Canada did not share.

Whether or not Justice Medhurst accepted this, his reasoning ran along the same lines as those of the American Court and of other courts which have heard similar cases: no democratic society can give one group a monopoly of expression; money is a form of expression; thus, all should be allowed to spend money in elections. Many groups resent and fear this bent in some of the judiciary, and the greatest proponents of advocacy group limits are generally incumbent legislators because they gain from any law that stifles electoral competition (Paltiel, 1988). Advocacy groups pose several threats; challengers may channel their spending through friendly groups to get over the official ceilings, and incumbents suffer because challengers usually get much more return for their dollar in election campaigns (see Chapter 3). A group may also oppose a candidate without prompting. In 1981 Jim Coutts stood as the Liberal candidate in the Spadina by-election. Coutts was to have assumed his place in Parliament in this safe seat as a reward for long service to the party. In pamphlets and posters, the National Citizens' Coalition tarred him as an *apparatchik* with a thirst for power who was stepping through Spadina on his way to the top. Dan Heap, a poorly funded New Democrat, defeated him handily. Perhaps in reaction, Coutts' patron, Pierre Trudeau, warned sternly that

> It is as well to remind them (the Citizens' Coalition) that there remains freedom of speech in this country. Anyone can get up and oppose any Party and any Member in any way. It is just that he cannot use the power of money . . . to give him an advantage over other candidates. (Hiebert, 1989)

Before the passage of Bill C-169, the Liberals had been the target of most advocacy group unpleasantness.[8] But all parties passed the law in 1983 without a squeak of debate.

---

8 In 1980, the Jewish Joint Public Relations Committee attacked Liberal candidate Frank Epp during the 24-hour candidate advertising blackout before polling. Also in 1980, the International Fund for Animal Welfare threatened to spend $3 million in Toronto ridings to oppose Liberal candidates to end the government's support of the Canadian seal hunt (Hiebert, 1989).

The challenging N.D.P. and P.C. parties may have done themselves harm by closing ranks with the Liberals because a law that favours incumbent candidates favours the incumbent party. If this seems odd, we should ask ourselves how likely it is that an incumbent would sacrifice career for the good of party. Long term harm to one's party must seem like a debatable abstraction beside the vivid threat of one's own political ruin. The incumbent probably believes his party is best served by his presence in the House. Otherwise he would have taken a different route in politics. Any act which maintains that presence can be justified on this ground.[9] Some American observers of Congress see in campaign finance regulation a cross-party conspiracy of incumbents to keep their jobs (Mayhew, 1974, p. 105). Jacobson (1979b, p. 101) describes how

> Members of both parties voted overwhelmingly for the Federal Election Campaign Act Amendments of 1974 [which restricted advocacy groups], the most comprehensive reform package to date. . . . The general effect of this and other campaign finance legislation has been to benefit incumbents of both parties.

Similarly, in the Canadian case "reforms have been proposed, designed and enacted by the parties in power. It should occasion no surprise, therefore, that the immediate beneficiaries of these measures have been incumbents, their coalition partners, and other major participants in [the] party system" (Paltiel, 1979, p. 19).[10]

The P.C.s reversed their position on advocacy group spending after the press took sides with the Coalition. Mulroney and other prominent conservatives apologized to their constituents and sang the virtues of free expression.[11] Surprisingly after all this stir, advocacy groups spent very little during the 1984 election and were not the centre of any debate.

---

9   Even party-minded members of the P.C.s and the N.D.P. may have wanted this law. Up to 1983, the P.C.s had benefitted most from the efforts of advocacy groups, but the intractable and aggressive style of the Coalition may have convinced them that the party's long-term goals would be safer with these volatile elements tightly bottled away.

10   Thompson and Stanbury (1984) found some evidence that the federal Liberal party has tried in the past thirty years to reelect incumbents to the possible detriment of the number of Liberal seats in Parliament.

11   This new position emerged in House of Commons debates shortly after the

The 1984 and 1988 elections

During their first term (1984-1988) the P.C.s let the matter lie. Advocacy groups had not threatened anyone in 1984, and were they to do so, the threats would probably not be directed at the Conservatives. Any hidden benefits of muting independent opposition was not worth a retreat from their public stand for freedom of expression and the threat of attack from the press and the Coalition (Hiebert, 1989). In the 1988 election the three parties locked in fierce battle over free trade. For the first time, advocacy groups became major players in a national campaign. The Canadian Alliance on Trade and Job Opportunities spent $3 million shortly before and $2 million during the election to champion free trade (*Lortie Commission Hearings*, March 12, 1990, p. 9) The National Citizens' Coalition spent $150,000 for the same cause.[12] The Pro-Canada network opposed them with an outlay of $600,000 as did the Canadian Automobile workers with two-page advertisements in major newspapers costing about $400,000 (*Lortie Commission Hearings*, May 31, 1990, p. 13).[13] In total, the Chief Electoral Officer counted 29 violations of the advocacy group regulations (Hamel, 1989, p.41).[14]

The N.D.P. and Liberals probably suffered most from these attacks and it shows in their hostile testimony to the Lortie Commission of 1990. They argued that independent opinion should operate through the parties or should at the very least obey the rules set for the parties.[15] Advocacy groups who had themselves been mauled said the same. The Ontario Federation of Labour told the Commission that unlimited expenditures by advocacy groups pose a significant threat to Canada's

---

National Citizens' Coalition trial began.

12   Related by the president of the National Citizens Coalition.

13   Most of these figures are self reported. The Canadian Alliance maintained they were the only ones to provide an audited statement of accounts to the public (*Lortie Commission Hearings*, March 12, 1990, p. 9).

14   Pro-life and pro-smoking groups were also active but did not spend nearly as much as the free-trade activists did.

15   See the testimonies of the Ontario N.D.P. (*Lortie Commission Hearings*, May 31, 1990, pp. 14-15) and of various M.P.s (*Lortie Commission Hearings*, March 12, 1990, p. 10) for examples of the many criticisms of advocacy groups.

political democracy. The Federation—a traditional supporter of the N.D.P.—claimed that the trade isolationists had held their ground in the debate before the election but that the free-trade forces had crushed them with massive expenditures during the campaign. The solution was to ban advocacy group spending unless it was part of the declared expenditures of a party or candidate (*Lortie Commission Hearings*, May 31, 1990, p. 1). The Council of Canadians argued that they should be allowed to distribute hand-bills and put out lawn signs, but that mass-media advertising should be the privilege of established parties (*Lortie Commission Hearings*, March 12, 1990, p. 7).

These are fine examples of the fact that no one likes to lose an argument and that each side in a debate tries to twist the rules in its favour. Groups that rely on volunteers want to stop groups that know how to raise money and how to promote an issue on the air. The 1988 election revealed the talents of each group and determined the side they now take in the question of regulating advocacy groups.[16]

The harm to voters of restricting advocacy groups

Many think it harsh to ban advocacy groups, but agree that they need to be regulated. The main argument for advocacy group rules is that money in elections threatens what Trudeau called the "principle of equality"—an extension to advocacy groups of the notion that no single established party should be able to outspend another. When Liberal Yvon Pinard put Bill C-169 to the Commons he said that

> The intent of the present legislation is to equalize the chances of all candidates in all parties, by setting reasonable limits on election expenses. . . . The basic principle of equality is unfortunately ignored at times by groups or individuals, other than political parties or candidates, that make substantial election expenditures during an election campaign without going

---

16   The groups who most firmly supported advocacy group rights before the Lortie Commission were associations of newspaper publishers and broadcasters, libertarians, and groups that had done well in the free-trade debate (*Lortie Commission Hearings*, May 8, 1990, pp. 4-7). Surprisingly, the Canadian Human Rights Foundation was all for regulating advocacy groups (*Lortie Commission Hearings*, April 10, 1990, pp.12-13).

through a candidate or party.... Under the Bill before the House today, all election expenses shall be made solely by the parties and the candidates who are running. (Hansard, 1983, p. 28, 295)

As pointed out in Chapters 3 and 8, this principle is blind to why any political movement has money in the first place and scorns suggestions that individuals can play a bigger part in politics than to cast their ballots. It springs from the fear that the rich will campaign to promote their own narrow interests. To date this threat has not shown itself in Canada and is not likely to.[17] Special interest groups try to stay out of public sight and prefer to influence government by lobbying in back rooms where none can contest them. If it must campaign, it is much better that an interest group should do so openly at elections where constituents can weigh the arguments and show what they think at the polls. In countries that outlaw advocacy groups it is easier for special interests to influence the government. The nepotism and decadence of the communist governments that fell in Eastern Europe in 1989 are perhaps an example of this.

The most important independent spenders in the free-trade debate of 1988 were not mouthpieces for businesses, but organizations that got their support largely from thousands of small individual contributions such as the Canadian Alliance and the National Citizens' Coalition. This fits in with the long trend of rising individual participation in elections. Advocacy groups give small contributors of the same mind a strong voice. These groups are agents for the public, who collect money and use it in a disciplined way to keep politicians in line.

Some ideas have too little support for a party to embrace, or are too fleeting to found a party on. Advocacy groups with low setup costs, little expectation of long life, and no need to please the majority, are their best

---

17   One M.P. attributed his survival in two campaigns, against a millionaire, to spending limits (*House of Commons Debates*, 1983, p. 28, 296). Millionaire candidates are the bogeymen of crusading legislators but the threat they pose to the public is not clear. One cannot simply spend one's way into office. One must be sensitive to the needs of constituents. Poorly endowed candidates may suffer, but the private advantages of the rich are probably well balanced by the resources that parties can put behind talented but impoverished stars. Recent millionaires have not fared well in Canada. Tony Roman failed in his bid for a seat in the 1984 House of Commons.

conduits. When loyal supporters of the large parties have a complaint they can send a message to their leaders at low cost through a single-issue group. Even moderate voters can use these very committed groups to their own advantage. Advocacy groups get their force from bending all their efforts to one idea. It does not take long to teach canvassers a single slogan, to devise a publicity campaign, and to learn how to use the press and fight off criticism from other groups. These investments in learning can last a long time. In addition, a single-issue group does not have to expend resources to reconcile differences of opinion and to avert strife in its ranks, as major parties are forced to do. An organization with only one goal does not have to tolerate dissent.

Does this power make advocacy groups a "significant danger to Canada's political democracy"? If we think of democracy as a system of government in which anyone can use elections to put demands to the state and contest its actions, then anything that makes it easier for all participants to make their case helps democracy. What is important is that all have equal *opportunity* to put their resources to best service of their cause. State actions that equalize resources or limit spending blunt the edge of movements that have found the public's approval, while giving a boost to voices whom most people were not interested enough to hear. Trudeau's principle of equality goes against the much older principle that a platform should get only as much support as the people wish to give it. Any government plan to "equalize the chances of all candidates, in all parties" goes against the public wish.

More benign sounding proposals for regulation can also do harm. At the very least, many believe that advocacy groups should submit to financial audit, and to other administrative procedures that large parties follow. This would impose large setup costs that many tiny movements cannot justify. Such methods are common in Europe where some feel that red tape has strangled new movements in the cradle and kept the established parties safe (Paltiel, 1980).

The benefit to voters of restricting advocacy groups

Perhaps a better argument for controlling advocacy groups is that because they are not accountable, as politicians are, and may be of very short life, they have no incentive to tell the truth. A campaign without them would be less distorted and more informative. Several answers to this important criticism are possible. First, politicians can advise voters to take the talk of people who will not feel the consequences with a very large grain of salt. Knowing what incentive people have to lie is an important part of being an informed voter. Anti-advocacy group advocacy groups—similar to consumer protection magazines—might enter the fray to warn about con artists.

We must also consider what "truth" is and make sure that we do not brand as misinformers, groups that believe in a different and less pleasant truth. Who is to rule that the shock literature of the pro-lifers or animal protectionists is a vicious distortion that voters must not see? No one is allowed to defame character with lies, but our society gives everyone their own rein to interpret the facts and to hear what others think. A law that seeks the truth in political debate must pass carefully over this slippery terrain.

I do not want to dismiss or belittle the danger that advocacy groups can do harm by convincing others of strident and perhaps mistaken views. But the world's experience of regulating the flow of facts to serve the greater good has proved unhappy and should give our best intentions at least a moment's pause.

Chapter 7

Should Contributions be Regulated?

Abstract

This chapter suggests why candidates take money and why individuals and special interests give it. Individuals can fight the lobbying power of special interests by letting candidates compete for their contributions. A candidate who is forbidden to accept contributions may pay less attention to the wishes of his constituents.

Introduction

ARE CONTRIBUTIONS TO CANDIDATES and parties in Canadian federal elections under-regulated? Canadian federal contribution laws are remarkably lenient. There is no restriction on the size or source of contributions; candidates and parties may take at any time as much as they wish from whomever they wish, and individuals, private and public corporations, crown corporations, parties, and even governments may give cash or gifts in kind. The Canada Elections Act requires only that contributions pass through an official party agent and that he report every gift above $100. A Colombian drug lord or a local criminal is free to send his cheque in any amount to the highest office holders in the land provided he identifies himself as the donor.[1]

Italy, Japan, U.S., Sweden, France, and Israel restrict the source or size of contributions as do six of Canada's ten provinces. Should federal contribution law follow these examples? The Ontario Commission on Election Finances writes that "Contribution limitations are designed to serve a distinct purpose, to maintain the purity of the electoral process" (1988, p. 4). The Commission shared the popular worry that big contributors buy out the candidate and recommended that to "inhibit corrupting influences in the political process by eliminating 'donation-for-favour' exchanges" the source and size of campaign gifts should be controlled (p. 5).

The purpose of this chapter is to ask whether regulating contributions ensures the purity of the electoral process. One can regulate contributions in several ways:

1. Limit the size of any one gift.
2 . Forbid big business, unions, and anyone else suspected of wanting a direct return from giving either money or material help.
3. Make public the names of people and institutions donating more than a certain sum.

Technical questions follow: what is a contribution? Money, gifts in kind, volunteer labour? What is large? $10,000? $100? $25? If a corporation gives on behalf of its employees does one consider the aggregate, or let each donation on behalf of an employee slip under the limit? Items (1) to (3) already guide Canadian contribution laws but some, (Hamel, 1989, Ontario Commission on Election Finances, 1988; Stanbury, 1990) have proposed ways of taking them further. They argue that the majority suffers when politicians reward special interests for campaign donations. Regulation should try to reduce such traffic but should not cripple the politician's ability to campaign.

In this chapter, I suggest that the majority may suffer more than do special interests from laws that limit contributions and that before acting, regulators should understand who gives and for what reasons. Certain special interests are small, well organized, and seek large re-

---

1   According to section 13.1(7)(a) anonymous contributions go to the Receiver General of Canada.

turns to their members by influencing government. They can gain influence by giving substantially to election funds or by lobbying their elected representatives at the seat of power. The average citizen, who may not belong to such a well organized group, can also contribute or lobby, but his best hope of making the candidate take heed is to contribute. No one person can find it worthwhile to lobby because it is a complicated, costly business in which certain types of interest groups have a comparative advantage. The voter's advantage is in contributing. The danger of outlawing or limiting contributions is that candidates will deal more with lobbyists and turn away from the needs of constituents who become good only for votes, not for money.

Limits on contributions: the majority view

Many reformers would like to put tight controls on contributions. In a brief to the Lortie Commission on the reform of Canadian federal election law, Stanbury (1990) wrote:

> For both philosophical and practical reasons, there appears to be a strong case for limiting the size of contributions to leadership campaigns (and to parties and candidates). "Large" contributions, by their very nature, raise the spectre of some form of reciprocity.

Fourteen years earlier, the U.S. Supreme Court observed that large campaign contributions harmed the credibility of Congress when given in exchange for political favours (Oper, 1986, p. 399).[2] The opinions of Stanbury and of the judges of the U.S. Supreme Court are widely shared: big donors do not give from deep conviction but because they expect favours from the winning politician. In Canada in 1983 and 1984, 28 corporations gave $10,000 or more to both Liberal and Conservative parties (Stanbury, 1986). In 1987 the Bronfman interests fed money through eight of its firms to give $116,292 to Conservatives and $111,873 to Liberals (Stanbury, 1990). If these donors had any type of conviction, it was probably that investors should not put all their eggs in one basket

---

2   This was part of a 137-page opinion in the Supreme Court ruling on *Buckley vs. Valeo*—see Chapter 4.

but should diversify to hedge their bets. Canadian and American regulators trust in contribution limits to chase such investors from the electoral bourse and perhaps even to broaden "the base for all political financing by obtaining funds from new, previously uninvolved elements of society" (Ontario Commission on Election Finance, 1988, p. 5). Public participation in politics might also be encouraged with tax concessions to small donors.[3] The remainder of this chapter probes the majority view by asking how severe the problem of selling favours for contributions is, and what unintended effects contribution restrictions might have.

Trends in Canadian political contributions

Trends in political finance over the past 16 years do not support the common impression that big business and other special interests are assuming a dominant role in the funding of candidates and parties. Table 7.1 shows that by 1988, so called "business" contributions were higher than they had ever been since official records started in 1974, but that they had fluctuated wildly: $11.4 million in 1978 and $11.8 million in 1985, $19.8 million in 1979 and $22.8 million in 1984. On the other hand, the value of individual contributions showed a steady rise in the same period, and over the past 16 years they sum to more than contributions from business (see Table 7.1).

These trends are meaningful provided the official definitions of "individual" and "business" really classify two different sorts of contributor. The Chief Electoral Officer uses the Canadian income tax code's definitions, and in practice, "individuals" turn out to be those who give in the range of $10 to $1000 to their party or candidate and who probably do not expect a direct favour in return.[4] There is much more spread in the size of gifts by business. The large spread includes many small

---

3   See the *Barbeau Commission Report*, 1966.

4   Out of 99,000 individual contributions to the Conservatives in 1983, only 45 were above $2,580. The average contribution was $118. The N.D.P. got a famous gift of $585,000 in 1983 from Irene Dyck (Stanbury, 1986—all figures are in 1989 values).

Table 7.1

Total of Business and Individual
Contributions to the Three Main Parties
Since 1974 (in 1000s of 1989 $)

Year	Individuals	Businesses
1974	$8,655	$6,025
1975	13,872	12,967
1976	—[a]	—[a]
1977	13,244	9,896
1978	14,963	11,463
1979	13,294	19,831
1980	15,192	16,651
1981	14,069	8,749
1982	16,561	8,065
1983	22,397	9,637
1984	24,066	22,844
1985	20,556	11,865
1986	21,324	15,194
1987	15,734	14,628
1988	23,888	26,798

[a] not applicable.

Source: *Report of the Chief Electoral Officer Concerning Election Expenses,* 1979, 1980, 1984, 1988.

corporate donations that are probably ideological and many large donations that one suspects are the price of political favours (see Stanbury, 1986, for details). The two categories, "individual" and "business," are not as distinct as their labels suggest—people in both slots may give for the same reason—but there are enough examples of businesses corrupting politicians and too few examples of individuals doing the same to make the distinctions real. This suggests that the dramatic rise of individual contributions is not an accounting illusion. It is the most important change in Canadian political finance of the past 20 years and it merits close attention.

Tables 7.2 and 7.3 show the details of contributions (in 1989 dollars) to the three main parties. Until the mid-'70s the Liberals and New Democrats got more money from individuals than did the Conservatives. After 1976, the P.C.s surpassed them both and received ever

Table 7.2

Business and Individual Contributions to Liberal and Conservative Parties (in 1000s of 1989 $)

Year	Individuals		Businesses	
	Liberal	P.C.	Liberal	P.C.
1974	$3,165	$1,819	$2,856	$2,786
1975	—a	1,396b	—a	5,374b
1976	7,612a	4,608	6,647a	4,628
1977	4,403	3,890	5,096	3,829
1978	4,293	5,458	5,089	5,372
1979	2,218	5,951	7,249	9,397
1980	4,232	5,446	6,336	7,422
1981	3,175	6,540	4,085	3,886
1982	4,345	7,038	3,435	3,985
1983	4,205	11,766	3,417	5,400
1984	6,386	12,543	6,590	13,587
1985	5,761	9,363	2,886	7,947
1986	6,575	8,970	5,527	8,330
1987	3,930	6,616	5,839	7,319
1988	4,987	10,696	8,870	5,074

[a]The Liberals only submitted a 17 month report from August 1, 1975 to December 31,1976.

[b]The P.C.s only submitted a 5 month report from August 1, 1975 to December 31, 1975.

Source: *Report of the Chief Electoral Officer Concerning Election Expenses,* 1979, 1980, 1984, 1988.

greater sums from individuals, whereas the N.D.P. made only mild progress and the Liberals made none. In 1981, 1982, 1983, 1985, and 1986,the P.C.s got more than half of their revenues from individuals. At the same time, the type of business from whom the P.C.s received money changed. Small, unincorporated enterprises became their biggest class of business contributor. The Liberals continued to rely on large corporate contributions more than the Conservatives (Stanbury, 1986).

Table 7.3

Individual and Union Contributions to the New Democratic Party Since 1974 (in 1000s of 1989 $)

Year	Individuals	Unions
1974[a]	$3,672	$383
1975	4,864	946
1976	4,313	812
1977	4,951	971
1978	5,213	1,002
1979	5,122	3,184
1980	5,514	2,893
1981	4,355	778
1982	5,179	645
1983	6,426	820
1984	5,138	2,666
1985	5,432	1,032
1986	5,779	1,337
1987	5,189	1,469
1988	8,205	2,855

[a]The N.D.P. only submitted a 5 month report from August 1, 1974 to December 31, 1974.

Source: *Report of the Chief Electoral Officer Concerning Election Expenses*, 1979, 1980, 1984, 1988.

It appears that the Conservative Party learned that with some fluctuation, it could take proportionately less from business, more from individuals, and still increase its revenues faster than the Liberals. Between 1974 and 1978 the number of individual contributors to the P.C.s rose five-fold. Between 1980 and 1983, the Conservatives tripled their number of individual donors and took from them two-thirds of the party's income. The trend continues to this day and is matched by developments in America where "Money from private individuals . . . remains the most important source of revenue in Congressional campaigns (especially for non-incumbents)" (Orren, 1979, p. 23).

The Conservatives were the first to copy American-style mail campaigns as a way of raising money. This was a big change, because previously, most of their contributions had come from several hundred corporate donors in Toronto and Montreal:

> Under this system, federal campaigns at the national and constituency levels . . . were financed from central party funds and sources. Few people were occupied in raising these funds. The usual fund-raising apparatus was composed of finance committees in Toronto and Montreal. (Paltiel, 1981, p. 143)

Over the protest of some M.P.s, the Conservative leader, Robert Stanfield, broke with the past and engaged a corporate agent, the P.C. Canada Fund, to plan the party's finances. He had to try something new because the P.C.s were $1 million in debt from the 1972 and 1974 campaigns. David McMillan, who managed the fund to the end of the '70s, visited Republican party offices to learn the new craft of 'direct mail.' The trick in direct mail is to know your audience. The party buys lists of names, professions, credit ratings, and personal traits from magazine publishers and specialist companies that do this sort of research. It then sifts through the list for good prospects. From 1977, the P.C.s systematically approached:

> small business people, members of the professional classes, and the intermediate managerial levels of corporate enterprise through the use of personalized electronically produced letters from party leaders sent to subscribers of upmarket glossy magazines and business publications such as *Report on Business*. Commonly couched in terms of neoconservative phraseology, these letters almost invariably remind recipients of the income

tax credits available for contributions to the party and its candidates. (Paltiel, 1988, p. 150)

The Liberals were slower on the uptake. They were a rich party until the late seventies, and saw no need to take a risk on the new direct mail technology. They could get their money from big business as they had always done (receiving sometimes as much as $100,000 from a single source), and from the door-to-door efforts of constituency organizations (Seidle and Paltiel, 1981). However, the Liberals soon realized that constituencies were no match for direct mail. M.P.s had little incentive to raise funds between campaigns because half of each dollar went instantly to the national party's account and because they could only stir local activists at election time. The party also saw that big corporate gifts irritated voters.

In mid 1979, Gordon Dryden, the national treasurer of the Liberal party, led a committee to study direct mailing. Several years later a second Liberal Committee embraced the idea and shortly thereafter the party made its first profit from the new technology. Despite these initial efforts, the 1984 campaign still left the Liberals $3 million in debt (Paltiel, 1988).

Reasons for the trends

At first, it appears as if the parties reached for small private donations because new technology enabled them to do so. In fact, the choice was never obvious. Until the mid 1980s, the Liberals and New Democrats thought they could stick to the old ways of getting money from corporations, unions, or constituencies. The Conservatives took the gamble, perhaps because they understood the details better, or perhaps because they foresaw that the well-informed voter of the near future would not trust a party tied to the accounts of a few big donors. If the Conservatives had this premonition, then the present has proved them right. Now politicians hesitate to accept big gifts, and representatives of each party at all levels wave the details of their finances in public and outdo themselves in volunteering to turn down large, suspicious contributions.

Conservative M.P. Francois Guerin has crusaded against the evils of accepting big contributions and has described with pride his ability to raise large sums from private individuals (Guerin, 1990). Trudeau once said, "We don't want to be indebted to any small number of large corporations" (Seidle and Paltiel, 1981). In this open climate, all three major parties have imposed their own internal limits on spending in leadership campaigns. Politicians and parties may be moving away from large contributions because it probably costs opponents less than it did twenty years ago to stir voters' resentment. It is also easier for public interest groups to exert pressure because "[t]elevision solved the problem of communication between interest groups and people in densely populated areas and gave groups the opportunity to mobilize a more general public reaction to political issues" (Thorburn, 1985, p. 15). Liberal candidate Jim Coutts may have been the victim of popular resentment stirred by citizens' groups when he ran for Parliament in the "safe" Spadina riding by-election of 1981. His former career as a party functionary with close ties to special interests was held up to view by the National Citizens' Coalition and probably lost him the race to Dan Heap, a poorly-funded New Democrat.

If it costs little to transmit information, then it is wise to take only honest, moderate contributions. In other words, the cost of secretive behaviour rises as the cost of publicity falls. It may also be that as Canadians have become more educated, they have come to demand a higher standard of honesty from candidates. Whatever the cause, politicians now seem to have a strong incentive to regulate themselves and to get most of their revenue from small private contributors who cannot exact favours for their support.[5]

Evidence that contributions buy favours

Politicians shy from the stigma of selling favours, but there is evidence that favours are sold. Reports from insiders give some idea of what

---

5 It is not always true that politicians have an incentive to be honest. This incentive, in politics, as in business, is strongest when two parties anticipate a long working relationship. In transient dealings people have less of an incentive to be honest (see Stigler, 1964). A candidate may not plan on being long in office, but his party does. Since the candidate's behaviour is important to the party, it will try to select candidates who will behave as if they had long horizons.

happens, but statistical studies also have something to say. In the U.S., researchers have tried to see if Congressmen vote for bills that favour their contributors. Large contributions come mainly through Political Action Committees (so called "PACs"). Ginsberg (1982), Johnson (1985), and Welch (1982) have found some evidence that the proportion of roll calls in a session of Congress in which the member voted in a special interest's favour was higher if the interest had contributed to his earlier campaigns. In Canada, Blake (1976) found that special interests in districts represented by government candidates got a greater number of government contracts than did interests in districts represented by opposition members.

Much research (mostly for the U.S.) is currently under way to establish a closer link between contributions and favours; the evidence to date shows some positive relation (see Bedlington and Powell, 1986). It is more difficult to say exactly how much of government is sold for contributions and to discern a trend. As noted earlier, contributions by private individuals have risen as a fraction of total contributions and this may indicate that special interest contributions are losing their influence. However, this does not mean that special interests are growing weaker or that less of government is being sold off. The next section expands this point in a simple model of contributions.

A model of contributions

Special interests strike deals during elections but they also reach agreements with incumbent politicians by approaching them at the seat of power. There are many ways to get a piece of the government "jackpot," a political contribution being just one of many possible approaches. Today, lobbying is probably more important. To put the importance of contributions in perspective, we need a model of candidates' behaviour that explains why they take money. The model presented here will suggest that a restrictive contribution law might simply convince special interests to shift their efforts to less obvious places than the election campaign, and may leave small individual contributors with less power over their representatives.

The model assumes that candidates may at times sell favours for campaign contributions. To understand why politicians take money, one needs to have some idea why they run for election. Politicians probably run for office with some plan of how they would like to use government power to fulfil their ambitions. A public office is powerful if the holder can dispose of large resources. The prime minister is more powerful than the mayor of a small town because the federal government has a bigger budget. The prime minister can also raise more money for his campaign because he can make bigger promises from the government "jackpot" to contributors looking for an investment.[6] But a candidate will not raise money just because the potential supply of available contributions is large. Money raises the chances of winning (see Chapter 3 on expenditures) but candidates do not like to exchange money for favours because every promise they make is a claim to some share of their power and because too many promises look bad to voters. Hubert Humphrey described fundraising as a "disgusting, degrading, demeaning experience" (Orren, 1979, p. 22). The ideal would be to get donations with no strings attached, such as donations from individuals (Crain and Tolisson, 1976, 1977; Zardhooki, 1985).

Candidates must balance the extra benefit of spending more to perform better at the polls against the cost of losing power to donors with great expectations. They will spend more in a close race where every vote could be decisive, or in a race for a powerful position where the benefits of winning are very large. They will not spend more just because they can raise more.[7] American studies (Abrams, 1981; Palda, 1990) show some support for the notion that candidates spend more in close races and in constituencies with large government resources. The studies also provide many examples of heavily favoured candidates who could fill a big campaign warchest but who spend little.[8]

---

6 I am assuming that the prime minister has more resources to auction for contributions because the federal government has a bigger revenue than does a small municipal corporation.

7 William Proxmire of Wisconsin, a long term senator, and Stanley Knowles of the N.D.P. are two examples of the type of politician who could raise a lot of money but who ran on their natural strengths, and felt no need to extensively fund raise.

8 American tests of the relation between available money and spending work well when performed across many states or (so-called cross-sectional studies). What they specifically indicate is that *at any given time*, an increase in the size of government will lead to more campaign spending. But over time, certain types of campaign spending in the U.S. have (until very

The model would be extreme and unrealistic if it did not recognize that elected officials do not control *all* government resources; civil servants have great discretion over policy. A sign of their influence is in the effort that lobbyists devote to courting the bureaucracy.[9] Table 7.4 compares Canada to the States and shows that in 1978 in Canada, 40% of lobbyists directed most of their energies towards the civil service.[10] Civil servants are more in charge now than in the past because government has grown faster than the number of politicians. The proof is in the lobbyists who do much of their business with a branch of government that is only remotely responsible to the people. As Thorburn laments:

> The traditional institutions of representative democracy are being bypassed as important political decisions are increasingly being reached through direct negotiations between government and important organized interest groups—most notably business and labour organizations, the related banking sector, and

recently) shown no tendency to rise (Abrams and Settle, 1978). The same is true for the U.K. (see Pinto-Duschinsky, 1981).

These two seemingly contradictory findings may be explained by the fact that since World War II the business of lobbying government officials has grown dramatically. Politicians may have decided to take payment for their services more in the form of special interest favours than in campaign contributions. The increasing public odium of big contributions may have caused the shift. So over time, campaign contributions did not grow even though the size of government has grown, because officials were taking their rewards in less obvious forms. On the other hand, in a snapshot of many constituencies (a cross-section) the political odium of contributions has been constant or "controlled" and has not drowned out the "jackpot" effect.

9   Ministers often made their own policy in the days of C.D. Howe (1950s), so lobbyists had clear targets. Trudeau introduced the cabinet-committee system in which ministers had to get the cabinet's approval for big initiatives. Trudeau hoped this would weaken the ministries and give him more power, but the result was that power seeped to the many bureaucrats who sprang up to help ministries work together (Thorburn, 1985, p. 11).

10   John Bulloch, erstwhile president of the Canadian Federation of Independent Businesses suggested that, "All positions that government takes are the results of conversations . . . between the experts who are owned by the major corporations and the trade unions, and the experts who work for government" (taken from Stanbury, 1978, p.195).

some other significant organized interests, such as farmer's organizations. (Thorburn, 1985, p. 124)

Government is like a big company with too few supervisors. Voters can prod the politician with contributions, but there may be little he can do to contain special interests who work through the bureaucracy.[11]

Why individuals give

As argued earlier, politicians may prefer the support of individuals over investors because individuals do not expect immediate payback. A person may give directly to the candidate or to public-interest groups such as the National Citizens' Coalition or Greenpeace who campaign for the candidate. The person does not expect political favours, but does expect the candidate, if elected, to behave as promised. No one contributor can hope to affect the campaign's outcome, but taken together, the contributions matter. This is why the candidate must heed the donors closely. People show how much they care about an issue or a party platform by the size of their gift. The candidate does well to keep his finger on the public pulse and to know what issues raise the pressure. If lobbyists on Parliament Hill offend small donors in large numbers, candidates will try to show that they disapprove.[12] It is important to remember that ultimately votes, and not contributions, are tallied at the ballot box, but money buys votes. This gives a large group of small donors clout, and keeps candidates alert to their wishes.

Many people donate exclusively to public interest groups. Such groups wage their own campaigns on a single issue, but sometimes give directly to a candidate or to his party. They are middlemen who present the contributor's wishes to the politician in much the same way that department stores present the consumer's needs to the wholesaler.

---

11   In the 1970s the government actually started subsidizing certain types of lobbies. Public advocacy groups received federal money, civil service help, and advice on how to start. Examples include certain native peoples' and women's groups. It is not clear, but the government may have nurtured these groups to compete with and interfere with the established lobbies in order to be able to control policy more easily.

12   Perhaps this explains the origin of Bill C-82 which calls for disclosure of interest group dealings.

Table 7.4

Proportion of Interest Group Respondents who
gave each Level of Government most of their
Attention

Target of Interest Group	Country	
	Canada	United States
Bureaucracy	40%	21%
Legislators	20%	41%
Legislative Committees	7%	19%
Cabinet	19%	4%
Executive Assistants	5%	3%
Judiciary	3%	3%
Other	6%	3%
Number	393	604

Source: Adapted from Stanbury, 1978.

Department stores seek out fine products and bargain with wholesalers for the lowest price. Their bargaining power rests on the allegiance of their many customers. In the same spirit, the public interest group gets power from contributors and invites each candidate to adjust his platform to the group's liking (see Sorauf, 1980). A person can show how much he cares about a variety of issues by giving to various organizations. In roughly the same sense that a stockbroker weighs assets in a financial portfolio to suit his clients tastes for risk and return, a contributor weighs his support for various groups and confronts the candidate with his own homemade platform or portfolio of preferences. For example, I may oppose abortion, and favour legalisation of drugs. This is an odd mix that I would probably not find in any one candidate. But I can give money to the Catholic Church and to the Libertarians in proportion to how I feel on each question. My ideas get freer expression than if I give directly to the candidate whom I think is roughly closest to my way of thinking.

Laws that limit the size of any one contribution make it harder for public-interest groups to represent their clients, the people. Quebec has very strong restrictions on who can give; in that province, lobbying is very difficult for public-interest groups (Massicotte, 1984). A limit on the *sum* of contributions a candidate is allowed to accept is worse than a limitation on the size of individual contributions because it makes contributors even less important to the candidate. Why try hard to appeal for money if you are not allowed to take it? Of course, if a limit obstructs individuals, it may also keep political investors from their goals since it is hard to buy large favours directly if you cannot give more than $1,000, and it is even harder if you are not allowed to contribute (Quebec provincial law forbids business and union contributions).

However, as the next section suggests, "wealthy interests" may have an "unfair advantage" not because they can make big campaign contributions, but because they can lobby bureaucrats and politicians at the seat of power. A large group of citizens cannot do this because the return it receives from shaping specific policies is usually small relative to the costs of organizing the group. Large groups are better at blocking policies (abortion, blockade of South Africa, stop dolphin and seal hunting). They can do this best at campaign time through their contributions. Limiting contributions diminishes the comparative advantage of public-interest groups and helps special interests.

How special-interest groups work

> [Fund-raising limits] would simply entrench incumbents further while ironically enhancing the influence of specific political action committee contributions. (George Bush, *New York Times*, July 31, 1990, p. A12)

Canada has many special-interest groups which make complicated demands on government.[13] The National Farmer's Union suggests a national land use policy; SNC Group and Machinery and Equipment Manufacturers Association of Canada call for Canadian content requirements; and the Association of Professional Engineers of Saskatchewan want a "made in Canada industrial strategy to be based on our strengths

---

13   For a detailed account of the size and activity of Canadian interest groups and their lobbyists, see the in-depth report in *The Toronto Globe and Mail*, March 10, 1990, section D.

synchronized to the world's needs" (Thorburn, 1985, p. 92). The simple motive behind their detailed briefs to Parliamentary Committees and submissions to privy councillors is to get control of resources that belong to the government or to other Canadians. [14]

Interest groups engage lobbyists to help them pick fruit from branches of the government tree. A lobbyist's talent is to get access to politicians. Access is "the ability to gain entry to key decision makers to make a presentation" (Stanbury, 1978, p. 185). If the client is a large contributor it makes lobbying easier because, according to Tory insider Dalton Camp, large campaign contributions "maintain access to the parties, keeping open essential lines of communication, corporate hotlines, so to speak, to the right ears at appropriate times" (*Globe and Mail* editorial, July 8, 1986, p. A7). Access means that public officials answer one's calls promptly and that one's case gets sympathetic consideration and the promise of further review by ministers (Stanbury, 1990, p. 13). But a donation is only one of many instruments in the lobbyist's toolbox. If donations are outlawed, there are other ways to pry open the government chest.

Some numbers put things into perspective. In 1978, parties received $12.5 million (in 1989 dollars) from businesses and unions. So it looks like some special interests invested heavily in contributions. Now consider this quote from Robert Lewis in 1978:[15]

---

14   The work of Stigler and Friedland in the early 1960s showed that most regulation in the States was not passed to improve efficiency in the targeted industries, but rather to redistribute income from consumers to producers (see Stigler, 1975). Olson (1965) emphasized that interest groups also provided their members with public goods, such as camaraderie. Peltzman (1976) and Becker (1983) later formalized these ideas. Their research suggests that regulators weigh the extra political support from transferring money to interest groups against the loss in support from consumers, or whoever is footing the bill, and that the regulator will be firm with the special interest only if it is easy to prod public opinion. I argue here that the cost of prodding the public has fallen and that a contribution law could wipe out the benefits of this technological advance.

15   Former M.P. Andrew Roman is sceptical of any estimate of the extent of lobbying because "writing authoritatively about lobbying is as difficult as writing authoritatively about the practise of espionage . . . the lobbyists are so discreet, so secretive, that you have probably never heard of them" (Roman, 1978, p. 212).

> Lobbying in Ottawa is a $100 million a year industry that assumes various guises: associations permanently on guard for the special interests of their clients, hired guns on special assignment and ad hoc groups who gear up for a specific legislative fight. If Canadians wonder why politicians never seem to listen to them, the reason is that official Ottawa is too busy heeding special pleaders to hear the unorganized. (Stanbury, 1978, p. 168)

Very roughly, in 1978, contributions comprised only one eighth of the effort expended to woo public officials. By 1989, lobbying had grown into a $200 million a year industry[16] and the ratio of campaign contributions to lobbying expenses was still one-eighth. This small ratio suggests that campaign contributions may not be the main thrust in certain groups' campaigns to win government favour.[17] To gauge the importance of these numbers let us ask how special interests—the "special pleaders" Robert Lewis speaks of—work and why their special pleading may get more attention than the needs of the general public.

Lobbying techniques

Sarpkaya (1988, p. 39) lists what a business must do to influence policy:

1. Take membership in trade and industry associations.
2. Maintain a public relations department to win the public or other interest groups to its side.
3. Lend executives to government under the government-business executive interchange programs.

---

16   Stevie Cameron, "A Question of Influence" *The Globe and Mail*, March 10, 1990, p. D1.

17   Stanbury's survey shows how important lobbying was twenty years ago. Of 176 companies in Ontario with more than 100 employees in 1971-72,

   1. 70% used the interest group approach to government.

   2. 61% of senior executives held or had held an executive position in an interest group.

   3. 33% reported regular contact with government.

In 1978, a sample of 703 Canadian firms showed half to be in touch with politicians and with civil servants at the federal level and 55.8% of firms with more than 500 employees made individual presentations to government.

4. Give to popular causes in a candidate's district.[18]
5. Present formal briefs to parliamentary committees, senate hearings, and departments writing White Papers.[19]

With luck, these activities can lead to informal discussions with cabinet ministers and top mandarins, where power rests. Businesses reward legislators and civil servants by:

1. Inviting them to company retirement banquets, ribbon cutting ceremonies, opening nights at the theatre, and other outings that mix pleasure with flattering public exposure.
2. Giving their children work in the company.
3. Giving them free use of company vacation resorts.

But businesses and other special interests get perhaps their biggest return from providing the government with information. For example, if the world pressures Canada to keep its tuna fishers from killing dolphins, public officials may turn to the representative of tuna fishers for expert advice. The industry is well placed to emphasize points in its own favour because it knows the details best. A skilful brief also wins the gratitude of the politician, whom it allows to appear informed, and of bureaucrats, whose job of drafting the details of policy, it lightens:

> The interest group offers information about people's preferences and agrees to support certain government programs; this assists the civil servant in his dealings with other civil servants. In return, the civil servant supports the interests of the pressure group within government. (Ontario Economic Council, 1977, p. 32)

A lobbyist also wants to sniff out budding ideas in the minds of bureaucrats and politicians. He locks on to the idea that favours his client and pushes it to the legislative pole position. Sometimes it is hard to say where policy starts. Andrew Roman (1978, p. 214) believes that the lower levels of the federal bureaucracy run Canada. A junior civil servant will draft a thought, send it around his department, and sometimes watch it float up past the deputy minister to the cabinet. The

---

18 Several years ago the CBS program "60 Minutes" reported that one Congressman on a defence committee invited military contractors to play golf with him at the cost of $5,000 a hole, to be donated to local charities.
19 White Papers are often the first and crucial step in moulding policy.

lobbyist wants to know what thoughts are circulating; he then encourages the ones he likes by offering technical advice and expert opinion.

Private citizens and public-interest groups cannot afford the cost of fighting the lobbyists on this slippery turf. It is hard to organize large public groups to monitor backroom deals because the per capita benefits are usually small. Public interests such as the National Citizens' Coalition, and Greenpeace are very much at the mercy of their member's willingness to send a voluntary contribution and many who benefit from their actions never send a penny. A private interest such as a steel worker's union is a smaller club where it is impossible to shirk dues and where the benefits of successful lobbying are big. It is not easy for the public to

> follow government closely enough to be able to take a really pro-active position to policy rather than reacting to decisions negatively once they have been made by government . . . it is sometimes difficult for those within the system to understand the various levels in the civil service and therefore next to impossible for those outside the government system. (1986 presentation by S.A. Murray before the House of Commons Committee studying lobbying—reproduced in Sarpkaya, 1988, p. 40)

Public-interest groups are better at blocking legislation than they are at proposing it. As the head of the Public Interest Advocacy Centre, Andrew Roman wrote: "Cabinet colleagues rarely had their arms grabbed by passers-by as they walked down the street demanding 'Where is that new competition legislation?'" (Roman, 1978, p. 217).

Parliamentary task-forces sweep the country for people's opinions but there is really no appropriate machinery to conduct debates with the general public (Doerr, 1971; Wilson, 1971). Elections are probably the best place to make noise and block special-interests. Politicians are especially pliant at this time because they covet individual contributions and public interest groups are at their best in exploiting excitement in the media to get the most out of their budgets. Both are reasons to exercise caution when regulating contributions. The next section lists further dangers of such regulation.

Further dangers of regulating contributions

The Ontario Commission on Election Finance (1988, p. 6) draws a clear picture of what is required so that no one buys favours with contributions:

> [T]he law must provide for valuation of goods and services, third party advertising, fund transfers within political structures, union check-offs, use of candidate's personal funds, disclosure of the size and identity of donors, inter-election contribution limits, prohibition on anonymous donations. . . . Reporting procedures must be periodic and take into account all assets . . . to maintain the integrity of a political system within a given jurisdiction, *ex juris* contributions must be regulated.

The message is that much more than contributions must be regulated to stop corruption. Third-party advertising must stop, otherwise big donors can simply spend on behalf of the candidate; "volunteer" help from large corporations or unions must be forbidden because gifts in kind can be as good as cash. Above all, spending limits would be necessary to plug leaks in even the tightest of contribution laws.

The American example illustrates how difficult it is to control contributions while not intruding on personal liberties. U.S. Political Action Committees (PACs) made mockery of the 1976 campaign finance law because of its concern for individual liberties. The class action suit of *Buckley vs. Valeo* determined that limits on campaign expenditures by candidates or by private individuals on behalf of candidates, violated the First Amendment's guarantee of free speech. No individual could give more than $1,000 to a candidate or more than $5,000 to a PAC, but a candidate could spend as much as he wished, and could accept the legal limit of money from any number of individuals or PACs. The law was not an effective bar. It merely presented an administrative barrier which clever contributors were able to overcome. A spending limit allows less restrictive contribution laws to be drafted because it diminishes the role of money in elections. What use are contributions to a candidate or party that is not allowed to use them?[20] But if contributions

---

20   It is possible that even with limits which don't allow you to spend all of your contributions, you still like the benefit of knowing with certainty that

are limited through this channel, costs of the type described in Chapter 3 are imposed (less political competition, lower voter turnout, loss of free speech).

The enormous trouble government has in collecting taxes shows how easily taxpayers can find their way around the seemingly comprehensive revenue code. If this is a good analogy, then it suggests that a contribution law without the support of spending limits must be very detailed and intrusive in order to work. For example, suppose that no individual or corporation may give more than $100 to a party. Corporations can get around this by forcing all their employees to contribute. Employees can be compensated by receiving a $100 'bonus' at election time. So if Northern Telecom asks $100 of only 1,000 of its employees, it can raise $100,000. If law forbids this type of group gift it may stifle genuine contributions that individuals make at the office. Another example is gifts in kind. Suppose I am a talented data analyst from Decima Research and that I wish without prompting to volunteer my services to the Conservatives. Should I be forbidden on grounds that I may in truth be acting on order of superiors who wish to send support under the veil of my volunteering?

Another type of intrusion is the requirement that contributors reveal their identity. As mentioned earlier, anonymous contributions to federal candidates or parties in Canada are forbidden; they go directly to the Receiver General. All contributions to federal politicians above $100 go into the public record.[21] Disclosure may lower the cost to voters of knowing which candidate is accepting large, conspicuous donations. However, if too vigorously applied, disclosure can violate the privacy of constituents. Earlier, this chapter argued that individuals can give money to show how strongly they feel about an issue. Presently, individuals who support a party or candidate with more than $100 have

---

at the next election you will have money in your warchest.

21 The Canadian federal law was drafted in the early 1970s and followed closely the American Federal Election Campaign Act of 1971 which called for disclosure of all gifts exceeding $100. The $100 level is not indexed to inflation, which means that with each year it becomes a more restrictive reporting requirement. Ontario is even more restrictive. It requires that the names of donors of all gifts of more than $25 be made available to the public.

their names and the amount they have given put in a public register; their choice of candidate is no longer private information. To get the benefits of disclosure without intruding too far into people's privacy, legislators must be sensitive to how large a contribution can be before becoming suspicious.

Another danger of regulating contributions effectively is that restrictions on liberty will grow as regulators try to close the trap on big contributors. Closing the trap will require a commission that can react quickly to new abuses without always having to appeal to Parliament to amend the Canada Elections Act, and which can prosecute offenses without waiting for complaints to be brought. In 1974, the American Congress moved in this direction by amending the 1971 Federal Election Campaign Act to set up the Federal Election Commission. The amendment gave the commission important powers to ensure that candidates gave clear and truthful financial statements. Shortly after, in its ruling on *Buckley vs. Valeo*, the Supreme Court dissolved the commission on grounds that

> the method of appointment of commissioners violated the constitution's separation of powers and appointments clauses in that some members exercised executive powers, despite being named to the Commission with the approval of Congress. (Ontario Commission on Election Finance, 1988, p. 121)

The Court feared that officials without a public mandate would be making executive decisions, that is, decisions that interpret how the law should be enforced.

Canada had a similar plan in the wings. Bill C-79 (which did not pass in Parliament where it was read in 1987) proposed a Canada Elections Enforcement Commission. M.P.s from all parties would run the commission and would consult with the Chief Electoral Officer on how to enforce the act. Commissioners could change the penalty for accepting an unlawful contribution, or they could take the power to search a political office without notice. They could

> obtain the assistance of the RCMP or designate a person to be an investigator for the purpose of investigating into a complaint. This provision would give the Commission flexibility to appoint investigators where it is felt to be sufficient and would give the investigators sufficiently broad power to do a proper investigation. (Ontario Commission on Election Finance, 1988, p. 48)

In sum, to enforce contribution law, it would be necessary to form a special political police with broad powers to expose and hunt down violators.

Conclusion

Contributions to a candidate can be a good thing. A contribution is the best weapon the individual has against special interests. It is true that these interests can use campaign donations to their profit, and their most successful efforts involve lobbying the government. Individuals do not have this advantage. Instead they can keep the candidate alert by dangling their dollar. Mass-mailing technology has made it easy to solicit individuals, and the falling cost of exposing suspicious dealings in the media has made it prudent to accept only small, respectable gifts. This may be why parties have rearranged their finances so dramatically in the past ten years so that now they get most of their money from individuals.

Too low a ceiling on contributions may weaken the contributing public's hold on the candidate for two reasons. The ceiling may stop any one person from making a very intense show of preference. For example, Irene Dyck gave a small fortune to the N.D.P. in 1983 and 1984. A ceiling of, say $1,000, would not have permitted this type of gesture. The more important reason is that people often give to public interest groups who use their accumulated money to sway politicians. A ceiling could easily hamper such groups because they often give large sums, on behalf of their many members. A ceiling high enough to let these types of gifts pass, but low enough to hinder large investor-contributors, might complicate the work of special interests who use campaign money to buy access to politicians. The worth of this ideal ceiling depends on how much lobbyists count on contributions and on access to elected officials for success. There are many ways other than contributing to entice politicians. Furthermore, politicans may be a minor target. Lobbies may pay more attention to the civil service because this branch of government controls so much. Contribution law would have a hard time stopping backroom deals between government and lobbyists.

Chapter 8

Publicly Funded Campaigns

Abstract

Governments fund elections by reimbursing candidates, by giving help in kind and by subsidizing contributions with tax breaks. The rules to qualify for reimbursement cannot usually be satisfied by small parties and tend to entrench existing parties. Tax breaks subsidize the political beliefs of contributors at the expense of non-contributors. Incumbents usually pass subsidies in conjunction with spending limits to contain potent challenger spending, and to lower the personal cost of winning. Public funding can make candidates depend less on their constituents and can reduce the information that campaign spending transmits to voters.

Introduction

MANY TESTIMONIES MADE IN 1990 to the Lortie Commission on election reform wanted government to increase its subsidies to political activity. The testimonies reflect the prevailing wisdom that public funding is good because it allows politicians to depend less on a few big contributors by bringing more private individuals into the financial base, that it encourages competition by allowing candidates with meagre resources to contest the established forces, and that it spreads "the burden of financing the democratic process more equitably among the governed"(Ontario Commission on Election Finance, 1988, p. 21). Such assistance would "reinforce the voter's right to know and to be informed of the policy alternatives and the candidates and parties competing for their favour" (Paltiel, 1980, p. 354).

In this chapter I try to show that public funding helps none of these causes and that it may actually do a great deal of harm. It tends to stifle competition by entrenching government parties, it spreads the burden of the democratic process inequitably by subsidizing some groups at the expense of others, and it diminishes the "signal" that campaign spending can send. In addition, candidates may lose interest in the needs of constituents if public funding replaces individual contributions.

The many drawers of the public chest

> By protecting parties from the failure which results from a lack of public enthusiasm for their platforms, public financing may make it less necessary for parties to respond to the real political issues of the day, thereby interfering with the effectiveness and responsiveness of the political system as a whole. (Herbert E. Alexander, 1989, p. 16)

One of the first examples of a campaign subsidy law is the Puerto Rican Election Fund Act of 1957 which protected civil servants from "macing"—being forced to give 2% of their salaries to the ruling party— by giving $150,000 to major parties in election years (Paltiel, 1980, p. 358). Since then almost every developed nation has followed suit. Governments pour taxpayers' money into elections in three ways: through direct subsidies to the parties, through gifts in kind, and through indirect subsidies such as tax-incentives for contributors. The next section looks at each of these in turn to try to see how theory and practice may diverge.

Direct subsidies

Direct subsidies take the form of inter-election maintenance grants and campaign subsidies. In Canada, Quebec has maintenance grants but campaign subsidies are more common.[1] The Canada Elections Act provides candidates who win at least 15% of the vote with a reimbursement of 50% of their election expenses (s. 63.1(3)). Regardless of vote, registered parties get 22.5% of their expenses back provided they spend at least 10% of the national spending limit (s. 99.25(1)). Table 8.1 shows that the subsidy to parties rose in every election to a sum of $5.2 million in 1988, but hovered around $14 million for candidates.

Who profits?

The main argument for direct subsidies is that they free politicians from big contributors. Americans felt this so strongly after the Watergate scandal that Congress decided to provide Republican and Democratic parties with up to $4 million (in 1974 dollars) for their nominating conventions, and to give presidential candidates $20 million for their campaigns. As argued in the chapter on contributions, no politician likes to raise funds. Subsidies may well relieve them of the "dirty, disgusting, demeaning" business of raising money *if they come attached to a spending limit*. Alone, subsidies may serve no function other than to raise the cost of elections. This follows from an empirical finding that also has strong theoretical support: how well similar opponents do at the polls depends on how much they spend relative to each other (Welch, 1981; Carter and Racine, 1990). If similar candidates get the same amount of public support none is better off than before; contributions still have appeal. Legislators must sense the need for ceilings because every democracy that subsidizes candidates also restricts campaign spending. Because challenging parties or candidates get more voter return on the dollars they spend, a subsidy without ceiling could prove disastrous for incumbents. It would be like arming an already dangerous opponent.

Abrams and Settle (1978) argue that the Democrats used Watergate to get government to pay for presidential contests in the hope of containing the fundraising power of the Republicans. In Canada, the big

---

1   Every year the Chief Electoral Officer of Quebec sets an allowance for parties in the Assemblé National. They may spend this allowance on party administration and on the vaguely defined activity of propagating their political programs (Ontario Commission on Election Finances, 1988, p. 102).

Table 8.1

Reimbursements to the Three Major Parties and
their Candidates in the 1979, 1980, 1984 and 1988
Canadian Federal Elections (in 1989 $)

Reimbursement to Parties (1000s of $)

Year	Liberal	P.C.	N.D.P.	Total
1979	$1,343	$1,485	$928	$3,756
1980	1,547	1,662	1,152	4,361
1984	1,746	1,768	1,309	4,823
1988	1,616	1,872	1,668	5,156

Reimbursement to Candidates (1000s of $)

Year	Liberal	P.C.	N.D.P.	Total
1979	$6,721	$5,363	$3,124	$15,208
	(273)[a]	(219)	(147)	
1980	6,215	4,881	3,204	13,900
	(275)	(215)	(152)	
1984	5,020	6,294	2,358	13,672
	(238)	(282)	(140)	
1988	4,888	6,358	2,981	14,227
	(264)	(293)	(170)	

[a]Numbers in brackets are the number of candidates for the party who received at least 15% of the vote and who thus qualified for reimbursement.

Note: All reimbursements are in 1989 dollars.

Sources: *Report of the Chief Electoral Officer Concerning Election Expenses*, 1979, 1980, 1984, 1988.

beneficiaries of the 1974 Canada Elections Act were probably the New Democrats. The New Democrats were a distant third in Parliament, but they had great influence in the minority Liberal government and were adamant supporters of limits and subsidies. At the time, the Liberals were the richest party and they stood to lose the most from such legislation. Their leader, Pierre Trudeau, may have conceded this important advantage to get the N.D.P.'s support for other government programs.

Although some parties may gain at the expense of others, the mix of subsidy and ceiling may help incumbent candidates of every allegiance. Subsidies spare all candidates some of the effort and obligation of raising money, but limits protect incumbents by containing the more potent spending of challengers (see Chapter 1).[2] Subsidies and ceilings can have an unexpected side-effect: they may reduce incumbents' obligation to constituents by blocking challengers and by giving candidates an independent source of wealth very similar to the private riches that political crusaders deplore.[3] It is probably true that an independent source of money frees candidates from some obligation to big contributors, but the corollary is that it also frees them from the small contributors. The perniciousness of this effect depends on how much special interests and individuals were giving. Suppose that candidates prefer contributions from individuals (see Chapter 7). On this assumption, (see Table 8.2) a limit will induce candidates to take less from special interests. With a subsidy, candidates will further reduce their draw from this source, but as the subsidy rises they will also take less from individuals. The final row of Table 8.2 makes the obvious point that a subsidy equal to the limit eliminates all contributions. The subsidy is simply reinforcing the "crowding-out" effect of limits discussed. The higher the subsidy, the less the candidate relies on constituents.

By the early 1980s reimbursements had allowed candidates to accumulate large post-election surpluses. Conservative leader Joe Clark

---

2   A subsidy without a ceiling would be a horror to incumbents if it helped challengers spend relatively more money.

3   Jacobson 1979(b) simulated the effect of the ceilings and subsidies that had been proposed, but never passed in House Resolution 5157, on the House elections of 1972, 1974 and 1976. He found that the package would have hurt challengers in 1972 and 1976, but have helped them in 1974. In 1974, intrinsic factors boosted the productivity of challenger spending making the simulated ceilings less of an obstacle, and enhancing the value of the subsidies. A high ceiling and subsidy is bad for incumbents because it may give challengers more than they could have raised, and lets them use these potent funds.

believed there was $2.5 million "salted away in constituency funds across the country" (Seidle and Paltiel, 1981, p. 274). Officials from all parties worried that these riches would weaken the enthusiasm of local activists for fund-raising and corrode the fealty of constituency organizations to their central party (Seidel and Paltiel, 1981, pp. 274-275). Few seemed aware that subsidies might also cut candidates off from constituents.

Table 8.2

Effect of Limits and Subsidies on the Contributions from Special Interests and Private Individuals that a Candidate will wish to Accept

	Dollar Contributions by	
	Special Interests	Private Individuals
Limit = $0 Subsidy = $0	$4,000	$2,000
Limit = $3,000 Subsidy = $0	1,000	2,000
Limit = $3,000 Subsidy = $1,000	0	2,000
Limit = $3,000 Subsidy = $2,000	0	1,000
Limit = $3,000 Subsidy = $3,000	0	0

[a]This hypothetical sequence of numbers assumes that candidates have a finite demand for contributions and that they always prefer individual to special interest gifts because individuals extract no favours. The first line of the table shows that before limits the candidate is able to get a maximum of $2,000 from individuals and that he chooses to take $4,000 from special interests. When the limit is imposed he will reduce his demand for special interest gifts first. A subsidy along with the limit allows him even greater freedom. Past a certain point, special interests are no longer a source, but as the subsidy rises he also starts to take less from individuals (because it takes effort to raise money). When the subsidy reaches the limit, he no longer takes anything from individuals.

Finally, subsidies degrade the value of the signal that large expenditures can send. A candidate may get many contributions from informed constituents who deem him a good choice for the constituency. In this sense, the simple fact of spending money can convey valuable information to voters who might reason that if the candidate spends a lot, others must think him suited for the public post. But if the money comes from government coffers, the act of spending may lose its meaning. The result could be a less informed electorate and lower turnout at the polls.

Specific grants and services

Specific grants and services are direct subsidies to certain types of activities, or simply gift-in-kind, of which free airtime is the most common. Canadian federal parties get free time in proportion to how well they did in the previous election (see Table 8.4). Other help may come in the form of free hire of halls and free postage. Britain gave roughly 8,000 pounds of this sort of subsidy to each district in the 1979 race (Pinto-Duschinsky, 1981, p. 233).[4] Canadian parties get some petty local patronage by appointing government-paid local enumerators (Paltiel, 1981, p. 167), but as yet they receive no aid similar to that of the British.

Who profits?

Gifts-in-kind may have the same effect as a cash subsidy. If a candidate intends to buy five minutes of television time and the government decides to give him two free minutes he will simply buy two minutes less, and use the money he saved for other activities. In this way he converts gifts-in-kind to cash-in-hand.[5] Sometimes, however, the candidate cannot do this exactly to his liking. If instead he gets 10 minutes of free airtime, he will not buy the five he had intended to, and will be

---

4   Subsidies play such a big role for British candidates because their spending limits are so absurdly low (3,050 Pounds Sterling for candidates in county constituencies in 1979 (Pinto-Duschinsky, 1981, p. 212)).

5   This is the same problem that plagues all "merit good" schemes, such as food to Ethiopia or public housing for the poor. Resources can be too easily switched from one use to another.

stuck with a surplus five minutes whose value cannot be redeemed. Of course he enjoys the surplus, but would not have spent the cash equivalent all on TV (similarly, consumers prefer cash to quotas because it lets them adjust their consumption more nimbly). This means that gifts-in-kind are not as efficient as direct subsidies in the sense that they do not allow politicians to get the same utility from a bundle of gifts as they would from the dollars this bundle would cost.

Such binding gifts may also favour parties who invest a lot in complementary activities. Suppose my party has many talented public speakers eager to share their enthusiasm from a podium. The free hire of halls will be of greater use to us than to any of our opponents who preach from radio or television. To us, public speaking, and meeting halls are complementary activities.

Subsidies to contributors

The Canada Elections Act gives up to $500 of tax *credit* (as opposed to deduction) to contributors, according to a sliding scale that favours small donations:
- 75 cents for each of the first $100 contributed.
- 50 cents for each of the next $450 contributed.
- 33.3 cents for each of the next $500 contributed.

Who profits?

Table 8.3 shows the cost of reimbursing contributors since 1974. The real value of subsidies to individuals rose, while that to business was erratic, but tending to fall. At the same time, the number and value of individual contributions outgrew all other sources of party money.

At first glance, it looks as if the tax-credit had expanded and repositioned the financial base of the parties, just as had been intended. More individuals gave because it became cheaper to give. It cost you $25 to send your candidate $100, $225 for the next $450, and $311 for the next $500. However, a one-shot change in tax credit cannot explain the persistent trend in donations by individuals unless one believes that it took people time to adjust to the idea of the credit or that successive waves of individuals came to learn of it gradually.

Table 8.3

Income Tax Credit for Political Contributions by
Individuals and Businesses 1974–1987

Year	Number of Individuals Claiming Credit	Credit to Individuals (in 1000s of 1989 $)	Number of Businesses Claiming Credit	Credit to Businesses (in 1000s of 1989 $)
1974	19,584	$3,641	—[a]	—
1975	36,226	6,177	—	—
1976	48,313	6,720	—	$1,116
1977	48,027	6,913	—	1,119
1978	64,527	7,958	—	1,332
1979	92,353	11,428	—	2,268
1980	95,547	10,844	—	2,120
1981	77,114	7,414	—	800
1982	85,941	8,524	3,507	771
1983	104,599	10,626	4,178	983
1984	151,308	16,849	7,561	1,979
1985	109,310	10,263	5,995	1,469
1986	117,566	11,325	3,979	953
1987	102,824	8,349	3,647	881

[a]Spaces with — are years for which this data is not available.

Note: This table is an updated and slightly modified version of the one in Seidle, 1987.

Sources: 1974-1981 data adapted from Seidle, 1987. 1982-1987 data supplied to the Lortie Commission by Revenue Canada.

The *trend* is probably due to the falling cost of raising money and the heightening political odium of accepting large contributions. In the early '70s, parties started to learn mass-mail technology. The biggest surge in the sum of individual contributions came to the P.C.s, probably because they mastered the modern techniques first. The tax credit was an incentive for individuals to give, and an incentive for parties to invest in ways of reaching individuals. But as with any new subsidies, the initial change in behaviour was probably the biggest change. Table 8.3 shows that the 1975 subsidy was almost twice that of 1974 (the year it was introduced), but rose little until the 1979 election. In the absence of a tax credit, a similar trend would probably have evolved because the methods of raising money continually became cheaper and because big contributions became a political liability. If it did anything, the tax credit gave the trend amplitude.

I dwell on this point because it is important to understand that a subsidy amplifies and redirects the driving forces behind contributions. If we can predict how these forces will change, we can see which parties will benefit most from credits. For example, the New Democrats depend chiefly on very small donations. If the type of person who gives small donations becomes more common, the New Democrats will draw increasing benefits from the scheme. If the distribution of income among people shifts upwards (more rich, fewer poor) a party that gets many $1,000 contributions from the rich will benefit most because there are more rich.

The tax credit enriches all parties but it worsens the condition of any whose *relative* wealth falls, because only relative spending matters to the outcome of elections. Thus, the N.D.P. would seem to have profited at the expense of P.C.s and Liberals and the P.C.s at the expense of the Liberals, if the tax-credit was truly behind the rise in relative N.D.P. (and to a lesser extent P.C.) contributions. The N.D.P. were certainly very keen to have the tax-credits written into law, and their leader, David Lewis, pushed the minority Trudeau government to agree to a formula that favoured small donations: "It was not difficult to predict that NDP finances would be given a significant boost by this part of the Election Expenses Act (Seidle and Paltiel, 1981, p. 246)."

A tax credit favours equally all who qualify for it, but it is also an indirect transfer of income from individuals who give little or nothing, to those who give much. If I give nothing, but pay taxes, part of my taxes will go to people who get the credit.[6] Some provinces choose to give tax

---

6   Tax credits are also part of what is known as "tax expenditures." Bruce (1988) describes the current debate over whether tax credits are analytically the same as the more obvious sorts of government spending.

deductions which are similar to credits except that they benefit the wealthy because a dollar of deduction is more valuable to people in higher tax brackets (Bruce, 1988, p. 39). Despite these technical differences, the unpleasant result of both schemes is that they force non-contributors to pay for political movements in which they do not believe. My public levy may find its way through the credit scheme to Nazis or to Communists, provided they are registered federal parties.

Public funding entrenches established parties

Campaign subsidies and tax credits to individuals bring unequal advantage to the established parties, which is why legislators fight so hard over details such as how fast the scale of credit should slide with the size of the contribution. But all established parties benefit at the expense of nascent ones. Canada is only one example of a country where the "serious" parties were in curious agreement on the general need for subsidies (even though they may have quibbled over the fine print). In Italy, Germany, Austria, and Scandinavia, the established minorities all worked with the majority to enact subsidies. Extra-parliamentary groups and small parties have fought public funding for fear it would boost the might of their larger opponents (see Paltiel, 1979).

Established parties are probably in such good agreement because fringe groups can be a painful goad to action. In Canada in 1984, the National Citizens' Coalition made this plain by raising a clatter about free speech in elections, which ended in the defeat of the third-party advertising restrictions set out in Bill C-169 (see Chapter 6). Such fringes force the established parties to take better note of opinions they would rather ignore.

Many observers with different political views see this self-serving facet of subsidies. Paltiel (1980) summarizes their thinking neatly:

> The major promoters and beneficiaries are the incumbents and the established parties. Direct grants are usually made only to those parties and candidates who have achieved a certain percentage of the vote, often fixed so as to exclude the "frivolous" or the "nonserious." (Paltiel, 1980, pp. 366-367)

In Canada, federal candidates must get at least 15% of the vote and parties must spend at least 10% of the official limit to be reimbursed.

Table 8.4 shows that this kink in the reward structure worked against candidates from minor parties, such as Social Credit, Western Canada Concept, and the Rhinoceros Party. From 1979 to 1988, the value (in 1989 dollars) of reimbursement to minor federal parties was $11,465. Paltiel goes on to say that

> Specific grants, such as broadcasting time, if allocated proportionately benefit the largest groups, or if made equally tend to favour those which have achieved at least some representation in the legislature. In either case, the established groups profit. Even tax incentives, which benefit recognized and registered parties on an annual basis and limit new parties and individual candidates to the formal campaign period, are biased toward incumbents. More significant is the tendency to entrust the administration of these schemes to bodies made up, or subject to the overview, of representatives of the parliamentary parties. Examples are the Ontario Commission on Election Contributions and Expenses, and the informal advisory committee established by the chief electoral officer of Canada, consisting of the senior paid officials of the parliamentary parties.... *The net result is a clear distinction between the established parliamentary parties and those outside Parliament, rather than one of size [my italics].* The

Table 8.4

Reimbursements to Minor Party and Independent Candidates in the 1979, 1980, 1984, and 1988 Canadian General Elections

Year	Number of Candidates Reimbursed	Reimbursement (in 1000s of 1989 $)
1979	31 of 578	$720
1980	8 of 653	190
1984	4 of 603	68
1988	12 of 693	193

Sources: Statutory Report of the Chief Electoral Officer of Canada, 1980, 1989; *Report of the Chief Electoral Officer Concerning Election Expenses*, 1979, 1980, 1984, and 1988.

grants tend to freeze the status quo ante except where new groups are able to muster new private resources and gain from an ideological surge such as a nationalist movement. (Paltiel, 1980, p.367)

At the federal level registered parties may in total purchase no more than 6.5 hours of the prime air time of any broadcaster of radio or television. Each party gets its share of the 6.5 hours in positive proportion to the percentage of seats it won and the number of candidates it endorsed in the previous election (see Table 8.5). No party may get more than 3.25 hours. In addition, stations usually agree to donate as much

Table 8.5

Percent of Purchasable and Free Broadcasting Time Allocated to Parties in the 1979, 1980, 1984, and 1988 Canadian General Elections

Party	Percent of Purchasable Time			
	1979	1980	1984	1988
Liberal	39.7%	35.1%	44.4%	22.3%
P.C.	34.4	36.7	33.1	48.7
N.D.P.	16.2	16.4	17.6	16.7
Others	9.7	11.8	4.9	12.3

Note: In all 4 elections the total of prime broadcast time sold to all parties on TV and radio was not to exceed 6.5 hours. Parties may only use this time in the 29 days before polling day but may not advertise two days before polling day. In 1979 and 1980, the Canadian Broadcasting Corporation (CBC) and the Canadian Television (CTV) voluntarily donated 2 hours of free television time. The CBC also donated 2 hours of radio time. Several minor broadcasting networks donated less than this. By the 1988 election, CBC TV and CTV were by law obliged to donate slightly more than 3.5 hours of airtime to the parties (214 minutes).

Sources: *Public Notices of the Secretary General of the Canadian Radio and Telecommunications Commission,* February 27, 1979, and *Circular #257,* February 18, 1980, of the same organization. *Statutory Reports of the Chief Electoral Officer of Canada,* 1984, and 1989.

free time to the parties as they wish. However, this time must be allocated to the parties in the same proportion as the 6.5 hours of purchaseable time, which means that no station can become the exclusive supporter of one party. Because advertising wins votes, a scheme that divides free and purchaseable time in proportion to past votes perpetuates trends in each party's vote. It gives more advantage to big parties and stops new but potentially popular movements from starting.

The many rules that govern the registration of parties and that ordain the way they are organized impose severe costs on fringe groups. Parties have to follow complicated procedures to appear on ballots and to qualify for reimbursements, and they must appoint auditors and agents to administer yearly financial reports. They now depend on paid professional experts to deal with the detailed instructions in the Canada Elections Act. Put differently, there are big administrative fixed costs to qualifying for subsidies. Only large parties can justify such costs because only they can anticipate a large subsidy.[7]

Massicotte (1984) argues that small parties were hurt most by Quebec's Bill C-2. This bill tied reimbursements in so much red tape that only effective administrative systems could work through it. Small parties disbanded between 1976 and the present partly because of the new financial regime imposed by the bill. Small parties lagged behind the established parties because they could not get at public funds. In this way, the bill turned Quebec into a two-party province (Massicotte, 1984, pp. 19-20).

Conclusion

Campaign subsidies to politicians are intended to even the chances for rich and poor candidates, but just as in the case of spending limits, they may favour the established parties. Political subsidies also go against the notion that a party should only get as much monetary support as the public is willing to give it. Subsidies allow parties to depend less on the desires of the electorate and thus work against political competition.

---

7   Paltiel (1979) believes that these overheads force parties to assume some of the administrative tasks of their constituencies, which strengthens the party and weakens the candidate.

Chapter 9

Summary and Conclusions

THE AIM OF THIS MONOGRAPH has been to examine the consequences of regulating election campaign finances at the federal level in Canada. The case in favour of regulation is widely accepted and is based on the appealing notion that without controls, the wealthy and the well-backed will buy their way into office and come to dominate politics. It is less widely appreciated that politicians may instead write campaign finance laws to stifle competition, thereby serving their own interests. The self-serving aspect of these laws is difficult to grasp without a clear picture of how money transmits information in elections, the link between information and political competition, and the effect of campaign finance regulation on the flow of information.

I have argued that campaign spending allows useful information to flow between candidates and constituents and that this promotes electoral competition. Challengers and advocacy groups use money to expose the incumbent's blunders and abuses to the public and to advertise their own ideas as valid alternatives. The threat of losing office for performing badly keeps the incumbent alert to the public interest. Any law that restricts the flow of information allows him to take greater liberties with the power and resources of his office, and such a law can be said to reduce political competition. Not all information is useful, but democracies provide politicians with powerful incentives to be truthful and to direct their information to those voters who value it most.

Of the many types of campaign finance regulation, spending limits perhaps do the most obvious harm to competition. A common finding in Western democracies is that incumbents receive fewer votes per dollar than do challengers but that at the start of a race incumbents can count on the support of a larger block of committed voters. A spending limit contains challengers' more powerful spending and preserves the incumbent's initial advantage in votes. A spending limit accompanied by a government subsidy to candidates is even worse because it releases them from their obligations to constituents, who would otherwise contribute money to their campaigns and expect a solid performance in return. Most contributions these days are small and come from private individuals, which means that subsidies, and limits on spending and contributions, weaken candidates' dependence on constituents and makes them easier prey to the lobbying efforts of special interest groups.

The complicated effect that money has on elections suggests that simple traditional indices of political performance such as length of incumbency tenure, voter turnout, and campaign spending, may actually say little about competition, voter apathy, and election costs. For example, long-term incumbents may survive because they pass laws to stifle competition, or because they do a good job of pleasing constituents; turnout is not necessarily a sign of voter apathy or lack of information, because even enthusiastic, well-informed people may abstain if they see no difference between the candidates; spending ceilings may reduce the amount spent but may actually increase the cost of getting information across to voters. Regulators can see through these confusing possibilities by focusing their attention on the institutional setting in which tenure, turnout, and spending unfold. Good campaign laws are those which allow candidates to learn the desires of the electorate, and which allow the electorate to exercise an informed choice.

This may sound like obvious instruction, but election finance regulation in Canada as well as in other democracies is moving in the opposite direction. The most alarming display of the tendency to control the flow of information is the present movement to restrict the right of private citizens to advertise on behalf of candidates. This movement has stirred opposition mainly because of the human rights in question.

Unfortunately other campaign finance laws that do not obviously threaten human rights and appear more like procedural drudgery can have just as great an effect on political competition. It is especially towards such laws which I have tried to draw attention in the present work.

Bibliography

Abrams, Burton A. 1977. Legislative profits and the economic theory of representative voting: An empirical investigation. *Public Choice* 31:111-119.

--------. 1981. Political power and the market for governors. *Public Choice* 37:521-529.

Abrams, Burton A. and Russell F. Settle. 1978. The economic theory of regulation and the public financing of presidential elections. *Journal of political economy* 86:245-257.

Alexander, Herbert E. 1989. Money and politics: Rethinking a conceptual framework. In *Comparative Political Finance in the 1980s*, edited by Herbert E. Alexander and Joel Federman, 9-23. Cambridge: Cambridge University Press.

Aranson, P.H. and M. Hinich. 1979. Some aspects of the political economy of campaign contribution laws. *Public Choice* 34:435-461.

Atkins, Norman K. 1990. Reforming the Canada Elections Act. *Canadian Parliamentary Review* 13:2-4.

Bhagwati, Jagdish N. 1982. Directly Unproductive, Profit-seeking (DUP) activities. *Journal of Political Economy* 90:988-1002.

Barry, Brian. 1978. *Sociologists, Economists and Democracy*. U.C.P.

Becker, Gary S. 1958. Competition and democracy. *Journal of Law and Economics* 1:105-109.

--------. 1983. A theory of competition among interest groups for political influence. *Quarterly Journal of Economics* 98:371-400.

Bedelington, Anne H. and Lynda W. Powell. 1986. Money and elections. *Research in Micropolitics* 1:161-187.

Bender, Bruce. 1988. An analysis of congressional voting on legislation limiting congressional campaign expenditures. *Journal of Political Economy* 96:1005-1021.

Blake, Don. 1976. LIP and partisanship. *Canadian Public Policy* 2(1): 17-27.

Bruce, Neil. 1988. Pathways to tax expenditures: A survey of conceptual issues and controversies. In *Tax Expenditures and Government Policy*, edited by Neil Bruce, 21-61. Kingston: John Deutsch Institute for the Study of Economic Policy.

Campaign Finance Study Group. 1979. Summary statements. *An Analysis of the Impact of the Federal Election Campaign Act, 1972-78*, Harvard University: The Institute of Politics.

Canadian Study of Parliament Group. 1990. *Reform of Electoral Campaigns: Proceedings from the Toronto Conference, March 1990*. Newsletter.

Capron, Henri and Jean-Louis Kruseman. 1988. Is political rivalry an incentive to vote? *Public Choice* 56:31-43.

Caldeira, Gregory A., Samuel C. Patterson, and Gregory A. Markko. 1985. The mobilization of voters in congressional elections. *Journal of Politics* 47:496-509.

Carter, John R. and Robert A. Racine, Jr. 1990. Relative campaign spending and house elections, 1982-1988. College of the Holy Cross, working paper.

Chamberlain, Gary and Michael Rothschild. 1981. A note on the probability of casting a decisive vote. *Journal of Economic Theory* 25:152-162.

Chapman, Randall G. and Kristian S. Palda. 1984. Assessing the influence of campaign expenditures on voting behaviour with a comprehensive electoral market model. *Marketing Science* 3:207-226.

Coleman, James S. 1990. *Foundations of Social Theory*. Cambridge: Belknap Press.

Crain, W.M. and R.D. Tollison. 1976. State budgets and the marginal productivity of governors. *Public Choice* 27:91-96.

--------. 1977. Attenuated property rights and the market for governors. *Journal of Law and Economics* 20:205-11.

Denver, D.T. and H.T.G. Hands. 1974. Marginality and turnout in British elections. *British Journal of Political Science* 4:17-35.

Doerr, A.D. 1971. The role of white papers. In *The Structures of Policy-Making in Canada*, edited by G. Bruce Doern and Peter Aucoin, 179-203. Toronto: MacMillan.

Downs, Anthony. 1957. *An Economic Theory of Democracy*. New York: Harper and Row.

Esty, D.C. and Caves, R.E. 1983. Market structure and political influence: New data on political expenditures, activity and success. *Economic Inquiry* 21:24-38.

Etzioni, Amitai. 1988. *The Moral Dimension: Toward a New Economics*. New York: The Free Press.

Ferejohn, John A. 1977. On the decline of competition in congressional elections. *American Review of Political Science* 71:166-176.

Filmore, N. 1984. The big oink. *This Magazine* 22:8.

Frank, Robert H. 1988. *Passions Within Reason: The Strategic Role of the Emotions*. London: Norton.

Ford, Gary T., Darlene B. Smith, and John L. Swasy. 1990. Consumer scepticism of advertising claims: Testing hypotheses from economics of information. *Journal of Consumer Research* 16:433-441.

Foster, Caroll B. 1984. The performance of rational voter models in recent presidential elections. *American Political Science Review* 78:678-90.

Garand, James C. and Donald A. Gross. 1983. Changes in the vote margins for congressional candidates: A specification of historical trends. *American Political Science Review* 78:17-30.

Ginsberg, Benjamin. 1982. *The Consequences of Consent: Elections, Citizen Control and Popular Acquiesence*. Reading, Mass.: Addison-Wesley.

Guerin, Francois. 1990. Note for remarks by Francois Guerin, M.P. for Megantic-Compton-Stanstead before the Royal Commission on Electoral Reform and Party Financing. Parliament Hill, Ottawa: Office of Francois Guerin.

Hiebert, Janet. 1989. Fair elections and freedom of expression under the charter. *Journal of Canadian Studies* 24:72-87.

Jacobson, G.C. 1978. The effects of electoral campaign spending in congressional elections. *American Political Science Review* 72:469-491.

--------. 1979a. The pattern of campaign contributions to candidates for the U.S. House of Representatives 1972-78. *An Analysis of the Impact of the Federal Election Campaign Act, 1972-78.* Harvard University: The Institute of Politics.

--------. 1979b. Public funds for congressional campaigns: Who would benefit? In *Political Finance,* edited by Herbert Alexander, 99-127. London: Sage Publications.

--------. 1985. Money and votes reconsidered: Congressional elections 1972-1982. *Public Choice* 47:7-62.

Johnson, Linda L. 1985. The effectiveness of savings and loan political action committees. *Public Choice* 46:289-304.

Johnston, R.J. 1987. *Money and Votes: Constituency Campaign Spending and Election Results.* New York: Methuen.

Hayek, Friederich H. 1945. The use of knowledge in society. *American Economic Review* 35:519-530.

Kornberg, Allan, William Mishler, and Harold D. Clarke. 1982. *Representative Democracy in the Canadian Provinces.* Toronto: Prentice-Hall.

Krashinsky, Michael and William J. Milne. 1985. Increasing incumbency? *Canadian Public Policy* 11(1): 107-110.

Krueger, Anne O. 1974. The political economy of the rent-seeking society. *American Economic Review* 64:291-303.

Lewis, Robert. 1977. The hidden persuaders: Guns don't make laws, but gun lobbies damn well do. *MacLean's* (June 13, 1977): 40b,c,h,i.

Lucas, Robert E. Jr. 1972. Expectations and the neutrality of money. *Journal of Economic Theory* 4:103-124.

Massicotte, Louis. 1984. Une reforme incaheve: Les regles du jeu electoral. *Recherches Sociographiques* 25:43-81.

Matsusaka, John G. 1990. The Downsian voting hypothesis: Evidence from California referendums. Manuscript.

--------. 1991. The economics of direct legislation. *Quarterly Journal of Economics*. Forthcoming.

Matsusaka, John G. and Filip Palda. 1990. Why do people vote? University of Ottawa: Department of Economics. Working paper #9004.

Mayhew, D.R. 1974. Congress: The electoral connection. New Haven: Yale University Press.

McAllister, Ian. 1985. Campaign activities and electoral outcomes in Britain: 1979 and 1983. *Public Opinion Quarterly* 49:489-503.

McKelvey, Richard D. and Peter C. Ordeshook. 1984. Rational expectations in elections: Some experimental results based on a multidimensional model. *Public Choice* 44:61-102.

--------. 1985. Elections with limited information: A fulfilled expectations model using contemporaneous poll and endorsement data as information sources. *Journal of Economic Theory*. 35:55-85.

McKelvey, Richard D. and Talbot Page. 1990. Public and private information: An experimental study of information pooling. *Econometrica* 58:1321-1339.

Medhurst (Justice). 1984. *5 Western Weekly Reports*, 436-453, Alberta Queen's Bench.

Merriam, Charles Edward and Harold Foote Gosnel. 1984. *Non-Voting: Causes and Methods of Control*. Chicago: University of Chicago Press.

Myers, Stewart C. and Nicholas S. Majluf. 1984. Corporate financing and investment decisions when firms have information that investors do not have. *Journal of Financial Economics* 13:187-221.

Nelson, Phillip. 1974. Advertising as information. *Journal of Political Economy* 82:729-754.

--------. 1976. Political information. *Journal of Law and Economics* 19:315-336.

Olson, Mancur. 1965. *The Logic of Collective Action.* Cambridge: Harvard University Press.

Oper, Felice B. 1986. Federal election law. *Annual Survey of American Law.*

Orren, G.R. 1979. The impact of the Federal Election Campaign Act: The view from the campaigns. *An Analysis of the Impact of the Federal Election Campaign Act, 1972-78.* Harvard University: The Institute of Politics.

Palda, Filip. 1989. Electoral spending. Ph.D. diss., University of Chicago.

Palda, Filip. 1990. What advantage do incumbents have over challengers? Research paper for the Lortie Commission on Electoral Reform.

Palda, Kristian S. 1973. "Does advertising influence votes?" an Analysis of the 1966 and 1970 Quebec Elections. *Canadian Journal of Political Science* 6:638-55.

--------. 1975. The effect of expenditure on political success. *Journal of Law and Economics* 18:745-71.

Palda, Filip and Kristian S. 1985. Ceilings on campaign spending: Hypothesis and partial test with Canadian data. *Public Choice* 45:313-331.

Paltiel, Khayyam Zev. 1979. The impact of election expenses legislation in Canada, western Europe, and Israel. In *Political Finance,* edited by Herbert Alexander, 15-39. London: Sage Publications.

-------. 1980. Public financing abroad: Contrasts and effects. In *Parties, Interest Groups, and Campaign Finance Laws,* edited by Michael J. Malbin, 355-384. Washington: American Enterprise Institute for Public Policy.

--------. 1981. Campaign finance: Contrasting finances and reforms. In *Democracy at the Polls: A Comparative Study of Competitive National Elections,* edited by Howard R. Penniman, 138-172. Washington: American Enterprise Institute for Public Policy Research.

--------. 1988. The 1984 federal general election and developments in Canadian party finance. In *Canada at the Polls, 1984,* edited by

Howard R. Penniman, 137-160. Washington: American Enterprise Institute for Public Policy Research.

--------. 1989. Canadian election expense legislation, 1963-85: A critical appraisal, or was the effort worth it? In *Comparative Political Finance in the 1980s*, edited by Herbert E. Alexander and Joel Federman, 51-75. Cambridge: Cambridge University Press.

Pammett, Jon H. 1990. Third-party advertising. Issue paper prepared for the *Royal Commission on Electoral Reform and Party Financing*.

Patterson, Samuel C. and Gregory A. Caldeira. 1983. Getting out the vote: Participation in gubernatorial elections. *American Political Science Review* 77:675-689.

Peltzman, Sam. 1976. Toward a more general theory of regulation. *Journal of Law and Economics* 19:211-240.

Pinto-Duschinsky, Michael. 1981. Financing the British general election of 1979. In *Britain at the Polls 1979: A Study of the General Election*, edited by Howard R. Penniman, 210-240. Washington: American Enterprise Institute.

Pittman, R. 1977. Market structure and campaign contributions. *Public Choice* 31:37-52.

Powell, G. Bingham, Jr. 1980. Voting turnout in thirty democracies: Partisan, legal, and socio-economic influences. In *Electoral Participation: A Comparative Analysis*, edited by Richard Rose, 5-34. Beverley Hills, California: Sage.

--------. 1986. American turnout in comparative perspective. *American Political Science Review*, 80:17-43.

Roman, A. 1978. Comments. In *The Legislative Process in Canada: the Need for Reform*, edited by W.A.W. Neilson and J.C. MacPherson, 208-217. Toronto: Institute for Research on Public Policy.

Rosen, Sherwin. 1986. Prizes and incentives in elimination tournaments. *American Economic Review* 76:701-716.

Sarpkaya, S. 1988. *Lobbying in Canada: Ways and Means*. Don Mills, Ontario: CCH Canadian.

Seidle, F. Leslie. 1987. Controlling federal election finances. In *Politics Canada*, edited by Paul W. Fox and Graham White, 404-413. McGraw-Hill Ryerson.

Seidle, F.Leslie and Khayyam Zev Paltiel. 1981. Party finance, the Elections Expenses Act and campaign spending in 1979 and 1980. In *Canada at the Polls 1980*, edited by H.R. Peniman, chapter 9. Washington: American Enterprise Institute.

Seton-Watson, Christopher. 1983. Italy. In *Democracy and Election: Electoral Systems and Their Political Consequences*, edited by Vernon Bogdaner and David Butler, 110-181. Cambridge: Cambridge University Press.

Sorauf, F.J. 1980. Political parties and political action committees: Two life cycles. *Arizona Law Review* 22:445-463.

Stanbury, W.T. 1978. Lobbying and interest group representation in the legislative process. In *The Legislative Process in Canada: the Need for Reform*, edited by W.A.W. Neilson and J.C. MacPherson, 167-207. Toronto: Institute for Research on Public Policy.

--------. 1986. The mother's milk of politics: Political contributions to federal parties in Canada, 1974-1984. *Canadian Journal of Political Science* 19:795-821.

--------. 1990. Should government regulate the financing of campaigns for the leadership of political parties? Notes prepared for submission to the Federal Royal Commission on Electoral Reform and Party Financing in Vancouver on March 27.

Stigler, George J. 1964. A theory of oligopoly. *Journal of Political Economy* 72:44-61.

--------. 1971. The theory of economic regulation. *Bell Journal of Economics and Management Science* 2:3-21.

--------. 1975. *The Citizen and the State: Essays in Regulation.* Chicago: University of Chicago Press.

Thompson, Fred and W.T. Stanbury. 1984. Looking out for No. 1: Incumbency and interest group politics. *Canadian Public Policy.* 10(2): 239-244.

Thorburn, Hugh G, ed. *1979. Politics in Canada.* 4th ed. Scarborough: Prentice-Hall.

Thorburn, Hugh G. *1985. Interest Groups in the Federal System.* Toronto: University of Toronto Press.

VanLoon, Richard J. and Michael S. Whittington. 1976. *The Canadian Political System: Environment, Structure & Process.* 2nd ed. Toronto: McGraw-Hill Ryerson.

Welch, W.P. 1980. The allocation of political monies: Economic interest groups. *Public Choice* 35:97-120.

--------. 1981. Money and votes: A simultaneous equation model. *Public Choice* 36:143-157.

--------. 1982. Campaign contributions and legislative voting: Milk money and dairy price support. *Western Political Quarterly.* 35:478-95.

Wilson, V. Seymore. 1971. The role of royal commissions and task forces. In *The Structures of Policy-Making in Canada,* edited by G. Bruce Doern and Peter Aucoin, 113-129. Toronto: MacMillan.

Wittman, Donald. 1989. Why democracies produce efficient results. *Journal of Political Economy* 97:1395-1424.

Wolfinger, Raymond and Steven J. Rosentone. 1980. *Who Votes?* New Haven: Yale University Press.

Zardkoohi, A. 1985. On the political participation of the firm in the electoral process. *Southern Economic Journal* 51:804-817.

Official Publications

Chief Electoral Officer of Canada. 1984. *Canada Elections Act 1984.*

Hamel, Jean-Pierre. 1979, 1980, 1983, 1984, 1986, 1989. *Statutory Report of the Chief Electoral Officer of Canada.* Chief Electoral Officer of Canada.

Lortie, Pierre. 1990. *Royal Commission on Electoral Reform and Campaign Finance.* Mimeo.

Ministry of Supply and Services. 1966. *Report of the committee on Election Expenses.* (Also known as the Barbeau Commission), Ottawa.

Ministry of Supply and Services Canada. 1979. *Report of the Chief Electoral Officer Concerning Election Expenses, Thirty-First General Election 1979.*

Ministry of Supply and Services Canada. 1979. *Report of the Chief Electoral Officer (Appendices), Thirty-First General Election 1979.*

Ministry of Supply and Services Canada. 1980. *Report of the Chief Electoral Officer Concerning Election Expenses, Thirty-Second General Election 1980.*

Ministry of Supply and Services Canada. 1980. *Report of the Chief Electoral Officer (Appendices), Thirty-Second General Election 1980.*

Ministry of Supply and Services. 1983. *House of Commons Debates Official Report, First Session—Thirty-Second Parliament.* Vol. XXV, 1983. Ottawa.

Ministry of Supply and Services Canada. 1984. *Report of the Chief Electoral Officer Concerning Election Expenses, Thirty-Third General Election 1984.*

Ministry of Supply and Services Canada. 1984. *Report of the Chief Electoral Officer (Appendices), Thirty-Third General Election 1984.*

Ministry of Supply and Services Canada. 1988. *Report of the Chief Electoral Officer Concerning Election Expenses, Thirty-Fourth General Election 1988.*

Ministry of Supply and Services Canada. 1988. *Report of the Chief Electoral Officer (Appendices), Thirty-Fourth General Election 1988.*

Ministry of Supply and Services. 1989. *House of Commons Debates Official Report, Second Session—Thirty-Third Parliament.* Vol. XI, 1988. Ottawa.

Ontario Commission on Election Finance. 1988. *A Comparative Survey of Election Finance Legislation 1988.* Toronto.

Ontario Economic Council. 1977. The process of public decision making. *Issues and Alternatives.* Toronto.

Regina vs. Roach (1978), 25 O.R. (2d) 767, 48 C.C.C. (2d) 405, 101 D.L.R. (3d) 736 (Co. Ct.).

United States General Accounting Office. November, 1990. *Voting: Some Procedural Changes and Informational Activities Could Increase Turnout.* Washington, D.C.